Psychosocial

MENTORING

In the framework of

Education 5.0 the Global Education Benchmark

Authors

Dr. Venkateswara Rao Mannem
Ph.D. in HRM

&

Mr. Purandar Sengupta
NIESBUD (GOI) Certified Master Trainer
HRCI & SHRM Certified Master Trainer & Facilitator
UNESCO Certified Facilitator
World Bank Group Certified Facilitator

INDIA · SINGAPORE · MALAYSIA

ISBN
Paperback 979-8-89961-743-0
Hardcase 979-8-89961-744-7

Honourable Chapter Writers

Dr. Srijani Ray
Assistant Professor of Philosophy
Dr. B.R Ambedkar Satabarshiki Mahavidyalaya

Ms. Mukul Kamle
Assistant Professor in Geography
Deshabandhu Mahavidyalaya

Dr. Keya Chakraborty
SACT-1, Department of Bengali Language and Literature
Dr. B.R Ambedkar Satabarshiki Mahavidyalaya

Shri. Suvankar Biswas
SACT-I, Dept. of Education,
Dr. B. R. Ambedkar Satabarshiki Mahavidyalaya,

1

Mentoring as suggested by University Grants Commission

**In the Manual "Deeksharambh" published by UGC, the nature of
Mentoring Function has been delineated vividly.**

The essence of mentoring function as specified by UGC is enumerated below;-

Mentoring and connecting with faculty members is the most important part of induction.

Hopefully, it would set up a healthy relationship between the students and the faculty.

It facilitates the student to
- ✓ explore oneself and allows one to experience the joy of learning, stand up to peer pressure,
- ✓ take decisions with courage,
- ✓ be aware of relationships,
- ✓ be sensitive to others,
- ✓ understand the role of money in life,
- ✓ feeling of prosperity, etc.

Mentoring takes place in the context and setting of universal human values. Human values as enshrined in our constitution like justice, liberty, equality, fraternity, human dignity and the unity and integrity of the Nation can also be part of this discussion.

Focus should be on inculcating values of equality and responsibility towards one's fellow citizens of any caste, class or creed.

Mentor-mentee relationship can help students form a bond with faculty members which can be of great help during various tough times in study courses.

Methodology: Methodology of mentoring this content is extremely important. It must not be through do's and don't s, but by the following methods;
- ✓ by getting students to explore and think
- ✓ by engaging them in a dialogue.
- ✓ by getting them engaged in group discussions and real life activities

Topics of Mentoring

The following topics may be discussed during the Mentoring sessions.

Day 1	Student aspirations, family expectations
Day 2	Gratitude towards people helping me
Day 3	Human needs of (a) self and (b) body
Day 4	Peer Pressure
Day 5	Prosperity
Day 6	Relationships

- ✓ Small groups of preferably 20 students with a faculty mentor each can be used for discussions and open thinking towards the self. Discussion on Universal Human Values could even continue for rest of the semester and not stop with the Induction Programme.

- ✓ A follow up in a later semester could even be considered.

- ✓ Besides drawing the attention of the student to the issues of life and their role in larger society, it would build relationships between teachers and students which last for their upcoming 3 to 4 years and possibly beyond.

- ✓ It is important, therefore, that it be conducted by faculty members of the University/College, the ones who would teach them.

Mandate for the Higher Education Institutions:-

1	improve the graduate outcomes for the students to ensure that they get access to employment/self employment or engage themselves in pursuit of higher education.
2	promote linkage of students with the society and industry to ensure that at least 2/3rd of the students engage in socially productive activities and get industry exposure during their period of study in the institutions
3	train the students in essential professional and life skills such as team work, communication skills, leadership skills, time management skills etc;
4	inculcate human value sand professional ethics, and the spirit of innovation/ entrepreneurship and critical thinking among the students and promote avenues for display of these talents.

Acknowledgment: Deeksharambh , Student Induction Program
University Grants Commission
New Delhi

***

2

Relevance of Psychosocial Mentoring in the framework of Education 5.0

(The Existing Global Benchmark)

Education 5.0 is the existing globally recognized standard of Education, which is characterized by the following features; -
- ✓ Personalized learning
- ✓ Integration of Technology with the learning process
- ✓ Emphasis on Psychosocial Competencies
- ✓ Focus on Sustainability and Ethics

Personalized Learning	The learning process for each individual should be structured in accordance with the perceived needs, problems encountered, cognitive proficiency, and learning styles of that individual.
Integration of Technology with the learning process	Seamless integration of Cutting-edge technology encompassing Artificial Intelligence & Machine Learning, Augmented Reality, and Virtual Reality with the humanistic elements of the learning process like values, scruples, emotional intelligence, social sensitivity, behavioral resilience, etc.
Emphasis on Psychosocial Competencies	Emphasis on the development of cognitive emotive and social competencies through curricular and pedagogical initiatives
Focus on Sustainability and Ethics	Education is linked with the outcome of achieving the Sustainable Development Goals.

Illustration of Cognitive, Emotive, and Social Competencies

Cognitive Competencies	Emotive Competencies	Social Competencies
✓ Creative Thinking ✓ Critical Thinking ✓ Decision Making ✓ Problem Solving	✓ Empathy ✓ Managing Self-Emotions ✓ Understanding the emotions of others ✓ Sensitivity to the emotions of others ✓ Managing emotional vulnerability of self and others	✓ Effective Communication ✓ Interpersonal Relationship Development (irrespective of Demographic Diversities) ✓ Sociability ✓ Ability to decipher the social needs and problems ✓ Spontaneity to contribute towards the gratification of social needs and alleviation of problems

What are the differences between the humanistic paradigm represented by Education 5.0 and the dehumanizing paradigm represented by Education 4.0?

Distinguishing Parameter – Principal Focus

Education 4.0	✓ Maximum emphasis was placed on the deployment of cutting-edge technology (viz. Artificial Intelligence, Machine Learning, Robotics, Big Data Analysis) in Education. ✓ The unilateral agenda was to get the students equipped with advanced technology and to get them converged into a technologically equipped workforce. ✓ Less emphasis was placed on the process of understanding the heterogeneity in cognitive proficiency, learning styles, personal attributes, needs, and aspirations of the diversified learners. ✓ All the learners are expected to achieve a structured Standard through the acquisition of Advanced technological skills.
Education 5.0	✓ Emphasis is on the holistic development of learners. ✓ Pedagogical initiatives are designed and implemented to develop the cognitive, emotive, and social competencies of the learners along with the intent of incorporating demand-driven technological skills within them. ✓ Instead of bestowing a homogeneity-driven structured curriculum upon the diversified learners, a greater focus is placed on exploring the unique competencies and learning styles of each learner. Accordingly, need-based and attribute-based personalized curricular and pedagogical initiatives are designed and implemented.

Distinguishing Parameter – Role of Technology

Education 4.0	✓ Technology was considered as the prime driving force. ✓ Emphasis was on the incorporation of technological skills indiscriminately upon the students and fostering their growth as data-driven and output-oriented machines, devoid of humanistic attributes.
Education 5.0	✓ Technology is being deployed as an Enabling Force, catalyzing the development of humanistic potential. ✓ For example, with the support of Artificial Intelligence and Machine Learning Experience Platforms are being created, where technology can foster personalized learning and assessment, by proper identification of the unique competency, need, and problem of every individual learner. ✓ Virtual Reality and Augmented Reality can play instrumental roles in fostering Experiential Learning. ✓ Experiential Learning is much more contributory towards the holistic development of the learners as compared to memory-based rote learning.

Distinguishing Parameter – Learning Process

Education 4.0	✓ Learning Process was entirely based on deciphering the essence of Cutting edge technology and eventually operations of Digital tools. Focus was on Cognitive learning viz. Learning was based on Memory , Attention and problem Solving
Education 5.0	✓ Learning Process is Social and Experiential. ✓ It is advised that learning should not be restricted to the precincts of Institutional building. ✓ Rather it is advised that learning should take place through exploration of the society, social Interaction and Community -Based Activities. ✓ Thus, emphasis has been placed on Social and Emotional Learning.

Distinguishing Parameter – Learning Outcome

Education 4.0	✓ The learners get equipped only with Science, Technology, Engineering, and Mathematical skills. ✓ The learners emerge as data-driven and output-oriented Robotic Paragons.
Education 5.0	The outcome-oriented agenda of Education 5.0 aims at developing the learners into sustainable and ethics-driven performers endowed with ✓ Cognitive competencies ✓ Emotive Competencies ✓ Social Skills ✓ Values, ethics and scruples

Distinguishing Parameter – Role of Educator

Principal Focus of Education 4.0	✓ The role of the Educators was primarily to induct technological skills within the learners, in virtual platforms. ✓ Since the entire learning system is automated, the Educators were mainly functioning as content creators and were responsible for uploading content into the learning portal.
Principal Focus of Education 5.0	Education 5.0 suggests that Educators should be Coaches and Mentors. Apart from developing the content pertaining to their specialization, they should administer Cognitive-Behavioral Interventions & Socio-Emotional Interventions to ensure the holistic development of the learners. The role of the educators is; ○ To foster the development of cognitive competencies within the learners ○ To facilitate the process of crystallization of emotional intelligence within the learners ○ To facilitate the process of development of social skills, social sensitivity, and social responsibility within the learners. ○ To facilitate the reinforcement of values, scruples, and ethics within the learners ○ To facilitate the learners in eliciting learning inputs from concrete experiences, through judicious deployment of Inductive Pedagogy.

From the aforementioned inputs it is distinctly evident that Psychosocial Mentoring has got significant relevance in the framework of Education 5.0.

In adherence with the principles of Education 5.0

Psychosocial Mentoring plays instrumental roles in

- Facilitating holistic learning
- Facilitating the development of cognitive competencies within the learners
- Facilitating the process of crystallization of emotional intelligence within the learners
- Facilitating the process of development of social skills, social sensitivity, and social responsibility within the learners.
- Facilitating the reinforcement of values, scruples, and ethics within the learners
- Fostering Experiental Learning by facilitating the learners in eliciting learning inputs from concrete experiences, through judicious deployment of Inductive Pedagogy.

***

3

Requisite Competencies of a Higher Education Teacher to conduct Mentoring

Concept of Competency

Competency may be depicted as the capability of an individual to apply relevant knowledge, skills and abilities for performing significant tasks in the occupational arena or personal domain.

According to the view of Prof. Richard Boyatzis (1982), Competencies are underlying characteristics that are causally related with the job performance of individuals.

Drawing the reference from the **Iceberg Model of Competency** (framed by David McClelland), it may be stated that Competencies can be categorized into two parts viz. Visible/Manifested Competencies and Hidden/Underneath Competencies.

According to the essence of the **Iceberg Model of Competency,** some of the competencies of individuals can be conspicuously observed or perceived. These competencies are manifested by individuals during the implementation of tasks. These manifested competencies include

- ✓ Knowledge
- ✓ Skills

The underneath competencies, embedded in the psychological framework of individuals, are enumerated below; -

- ✓ Motives (the factors which trigger a drive within individuals to execute tasks and achieve the desired outcome)
- ✓ Psychological Traits (the psychological characteristic features of individuals)
- ✓ Self -Image (how an individual view himself)
- ✓ Social Roles (how an individual perceives different roles played by different individuals in the social framework)

The concentration /intensity of the underneath psychological competencies (viz. Motives, Traits, Self-Image, and Social Role) is much larger than the concentration/intensity of the manifested competencies (viz. Skill & Knowledge).

It can be inferred that the underneath competencies (viz. Motives, Psychological Traits, Self-Image & Social Role) have a direct influence upon the manifested competencies (viz. Knowledge and Skill).

Requisite Competencies of a Facilitator

To conduct Facilitation viz. to administer facilitating interventions, a Higher Education Teacher should be endowed with a bouquet of psycho-social competencies as well as functional competencies .

Psycho-social competencies are basically the psychological traits in the Competency Structure. Functional Competencies mainly cover the domain specific knowledge and skills viz. the manifested part in the Competency Structure.

Let us concentrate on the Psychosocial Competencies that are highly required for a Faculty to conduct Facilitation.

Requisite Psychosocial Competencies	Brief Description from the beneficial perspective
Creative Thinking	Ability to generate exclusive, innovative, and unprecedented ideas
Critical thinking	Ability to analyse and evaluate theoretical topics as well as practical projects
Decision Making	Ability to take a smart decision at the right time and appropriate situation
Problem-Solving	✓ Ability to trace out the root cause/fundamental causative factor of different problems ✓ Ability to dilute the causative factors ✓ Ability to solve problems
Effective Communication	✓ Ability to maintain two-way communication with others ✓ Ability to frame and deliver content that can be comprehended by the target- audience ✓ Ability to frame and deliver content that has situational relevance ✓ Ability to frame and deliver content that is emotionally supportive to others ✓ Ability to execute Probing & Paraphrasing
Relationship Development	Ability to establish mutually beneficial and reciprocally supportive relationships with the learners
Empathy	The ability of the Facilitator to perceive the problems of the learners as if those are his/her own problems
Managing Stress	✓ Ability to identify the factors that trigger stress within the learners ✓ Facilitating the learners to dilute the causative factors triggering stress

	✓ Ability to steer the thought process of the learners in a positive direction with an optimistic approach .
Emotional intelligence	✓ Ability to identify his/her own emotions ✓ Ability to regulate and deploy emotions in the most judicious pattern ✓ Ability to comprehend the emotive status of the learners and treat the learners with empathetic sensitivity

Now let us concentrate on the requisite Functional Competencies of the Teachers that are instrumental to conduct Facilitation

Requisite Functional Competencies	Brief Description of Features from the beneficial perspective
Ability to Facilitate by CASES & SUCCESS STORIES	It includes: - ✓ Flair of narrating Cases and Success Stories with eloquence ✓ Ability to explain the Critical Success Factors and the Contingencies embedded in the Cases and Success Stories ✓ Capability to induce Achievement Motivation within the learners ✓ Capacity to facilitate the learners in comprehending the Success Stories, eliciting their essence, and drawing the logical inference
Ability to Facilitate by ROLE PLAYS	It includes: - ✓ Ability to design Role Plays on the basis of the relevant situational factors ✓ Capability to select the right /appropriate role for each learner depending upon the personality of each of them ✓ Proficiency to motivate the learners in enacting the roles allotted to them ✓ Ability to facilitate the learners in understanding the relationship between situational factors and the thematic components of the Role Play. ✓ Expertise to facilitate the learners in deciphering the complexities of learning inputs through the proceedings of the Role Play ✓ Competence to facilitate the learners in drawing logical inferences regarding the thematic and operational aspects of Role Play

Ability to execute Scaffolding / provide learning guidance	It includes: - ✓ The capability of inducting new skills /concepts to the novice learners ✓ The competence to identify the gap between what the novice learners can do alone and how much they can accomplish under the guidance of the expert Facilitator (viz. the Zone of Proximal Development) ✓ Capability of providing instrumental support and active guidance to novice learners for implementing specific tasks that they have not performed before ✓ Expertise to support novice learners diligently until they become capable of implementing the tasks independently
Ability to motivate learners through Positive Reinforcement	It includes: - ✓ Ability to determine the desired behavior expected from the learners ✓ Capability of motivating the learners to execute the desired behavior. ✓ Proficiency to administer reinforcing stimulus (appreciation / acknowledgment /award) for motivating the learners to repeat the execution of each desired behavior with greater frequency
Ability to conduct Inquiry-based Teaching model	It includes: - ✓ Ability to float queries relevant to the topic of learning ✓ Flair of motivating the learners for responding to the queries ✓ Ability to administer Probing techniques for eliciting the desired response from the learners ✓ Capacity to facilitate the learners in unleashing their pent-up creative potential ✓ Capability of facilitating the learners to solve problems by motivating them to apply their creativity, insight, and intuition. ✓ Proficiency in fostering meta-cognitive competency within the learners so that they can identify the thought inducing another thought and the thought promoting every action.

Ability to foster Collaborative learning	It includes: - ✓ The Facilitator's competency to integrate the learners with a common learning goal, ✓ Capability of motivating the learners to create a common learning path leading towards the achievement of the common learning goal. ✓ Proficiency to facilitate the learners in exchanging their views and opinions with each other ✓ Capacity to empower the learners by the acquisition of valued inputs from the peers ✓ Flair to foster knowledge development within the learners by encouraging extensive social interaction among the learners
Ability to deploy digital tools	It includes; - ✓ Conceptual clarity regarding the rationale and justification of digital tools in the educational sector ✓ Capability of illustrating and explaining the salient features of different digital tools ✓ Proficiency in judicious application of digital tools ✓ Capability of analyzing the pros and cons of different digital tools ✓ Competency in executing comparative analysis among the different digital tools of similar category
Ability to demonstrate technical skill in lab/live learning/dem onstration	It includes: - ✓ Ability to explain a lesson or solve a problem by demonstrating technical skills ✓ Capability to empower the learners in comprehending the logical sequence of the demonstration process. ✓ Competence to guide the learners in replicating the demonstrated process with accuracy
Ability to replenish the learning gap	It includes: - ✓ The capability of the Facilitator to execute an interim assessment ✓ The competence of the Facilitator to detect the gap between the expected learning outcome and the achieved learning outcome at every milestone in the learning process ✓ Proficiency of the Facilitator to design and implement the appropriate Instructional Strategies for replenishing the detected gap in learning outcome

Ability to create	It includes: - ✓ The Facilitators' competence to identify the situational factors that can empower the learners in comprehending analyzing and evaluating the learning inputs ✓ The proficiency of the Facilitator to identify the situational factors that can ensure the ease and comfort of the learners ✓ The capability of the Facilitator to incorporate the aforementioned conducive factors in the learning session, which will ensure the cognitive and emotive empowerment of the learners

Now let us find how the some significant psychosocial and functional competencies, (that are instrumental for conducting Facilitation), can exert beneficial impact upon the comprehension and application of the learners.

Impact of selected Psycho-social competencies on the Comprehension and Application of the learners

Psychosocial Competency	Impact upon the understanding process of the learners	Impact upon the application process of the learners
Ability of Creative Problem Solving	The learners will be able to: ✓ Comprehend the concept, and paradigm of creative problem solving ✓ Understand the logical rationale for administering creative problem-solving methodology ✓ Comprehend the process of creative problem-solving through diversified tools, and methods ✓ Comprehend the differences between the creative problem-solving model, and the traditional model of problem-solving through analytical thinking ✓ Perceive the beneficial ✓ outcome of creative problem-solving	The learners will be able to: ✓ Alleviate complex problems by deploying tools, and methods of creativity-driven problem solving, under the guidance of the instructor ✓ After incurring greater experiential learning, the learners will be able to solve complex problems, by independent deployment of tools, and methods of creativity-driven problem-solving,

Psychosocial Competency	Impact upon the understanding process of the learners	Impact upon the application process of the learners
Ability to empathize with the problems of learners	The learners will be able to: ✓ Perceive the immense significance of empathy in human life ✓ Internalize empathy, and get it embedded within their value system ✓ Achieve emotional enrichment	The learners will be able to: ✓ Empathize deeply with the problems of the peer learners ✓ Empathize deeply with the problems of the known people ✓ Empathize deeply with the problems of unknown people

Psychosocial Competency	Impact upon the understanding process of the learners	Impact upon the application process of the learners
Ability to think in a Critical & Structured pattern	The learners will be able to: ✓ Comprehend the rationale of structured thinking in the sphere of learning ✓ Comprehend the mechanism of structured thinking	The learners will be able to: ✓ Generate structured concepts, and views without any ambiguity ✓ Entwine the different relevant components, and develop a holistic, and integrated paradigm ✓ Segregate complex problems into small simpler components ✓ Alleviate each of the smaller simple problem components ✓ separately

Instrumental impact of Functional Competencies , that are pivotal for conducting facilitation , upon the comprehension and Application of the Learners

Functional Competency	Impact upon the understanding process of the learners	Impact upon the application process of the learners
Ability to design and implement **Inductive Pedagogical Interventions** like Design Thinking , Mind Mapping , Force Field Analysis	The learners will ✓ incur concrete experience ✓ reflect deeply on the incurred experience ✓ develop abstract concept as an outcome of reflection	The learners will ✓ carry out Active Experimentation of the abstract concept ✓ incur concrete experience ✓ elicit learning inputs from the incurred experiences.

Functional Competency	Impact upon the understanding process of the learners	Impact upon the application process of the learners
Ability to facilitate by Cases & Success stories	The learners will be able to ✓ Comprehend the logical rationale of the motivational cases & success stories in the sphere of learning ✓ Understand the cause-effect relationship between effort and performance enhancement ✓ Understand the cause-effect dynamics between high-quality performance and beneficial outcome	The learners will be able to: ✓ Initiate behavioral modelling by replicating the outcome-oriented performance of the central character/protagonist of the success story. ✓ Design outcome-oriented action plans ✓ Elicit, and utilize their resources for implementing the result-oriented action plans with the valued intent of achieving the outcome

Functional Competency	Impact upon the understanding process of the learners	Impact upon the application process of the learners
Ability to facilitate by Role- Plays	The learners will be able to comprehend: ✓ The significance of role-play in elucidating complex theme ✓ The significance of role-play in enhancing the proficiency ✓ of verbal communication	The learners will be able to: ✓ Ensure their spontaneity- driven active participation in role-plays ✓ Enact their allotted roles with precision and finesse ✓ Incur practical experiences ✓ while enacting the roles, and
	✓ The significance of role-play in inducing collaborative learning	Retrieving learning inputs from incurred experiences. Thus, the learners will get enriched by experiential learning ✓ Communicate, and collaborate with the other role-players ✓ Get engaged in the collaborative learning process during the implementation of role-plays

Functional Competency	Impact upon the understanding process of the learners	Impact upon the application process of the learners
Ability to execute scaffolding /provide learning guidance	The learners will be able to: ✓ Understand the logical rationale of scaffolding in the sphere of learning ✓ Comprehend the mechanism of scaffolding, with all its intricacies ✓ Understand the beneficial outcome of scaffolding, especially during the acquisition, and implementation of new learning inputs	The learners will be able to: ✓ Ensure seamless acquisition, and implementation of newly learned concepts, and skills under the active support of the instructor ✓ Identify, and analyze the procedural deviations during the implementation of the task. ✓ Replenish the process gap/ deviations by administering need- based strategic interventions, under the valued guidance of the instructor

Functional Competency	Impact upon the understanding process of the learners	Impact upon the application process of the learners
Ability to motivate learners through positive reinforcement	The learners will be able to: ✓ Comprehend the logical rationale of positive reinforcement in the sphere of learning ✓ Understand the cause-effect relationship between the desired performance of the learners, and the positive reinforcing stimuli administered by the trainer ✓ Understand the cause-effect relationship between the positive reinforcing stimuli administered by the trainer, and the frequent repetition of appreciable performance of the learners	The learners will be able to: ✓ Enhance the frequency of their appreciable performance as an outcome of the reinforcing stimuli received from the trainer (in the form of appreciation award, and acknowledgement) ✓ Convert the appreciated behaviour into sustained habit under the influence of continually administered positive reinforcing stimuli.

Functional Competency	Impact upon the understanding process of the learners	Impact upon the application process of the learners
Ability to conduct inquiry-based facilitation model	The learners will be able to: ✓ Understand the rationale, process, and beneficial outcome of inquiry-based facilitation ✓ Understand the cause-effect relationship between inquiry-based facilitation, and discovery learning	The learners will be able to: ✓ Ventilate spontaneous response to the queries floated by the trainer ✓ Introspect, identify, and unleash their latent competencies ✓ Leverage their past knowledge, and experience for solving the present problems ✓ Mitigate the problems presented by the trainer, through the prompt application of their intrinsic creativity, imagination, and insight.

Functional Competency	Impact upon the understanding process of the learners	Impact upon the application process of the learners
Ability to foster collaborative learning	The learners will be able to: ✓ Construe the logical rationale of collaborative learning ✓ Comprehend the mechanism of collaborative learning associated with enhanced socialization, and resultant solidarity among the learners ✓ Perceive the beneficial role of the collaborative learning model in enhancing the momentum of learning process, and fortifying rational-emotive acumen of the learners.	The learners will be able to: ✓ Interact with each other spontaneously ✓ Integrate their valued ideas, and form a cohesive paradigm ✓ Share, and exchange their views, and opinions with the peer learners. ✓ Orchestrate the peer-to- peer learning among themselves ✓ Achieve their common learning goal through their combined, concerted, and ✓ collaborative, and effort.

Functional Competency	Impact upon the understanding process of the learners	Impact upon the application process of the learners
Ability to demonstrate technical skills	The learners will be able to: ✓ Observe the intricacies of the demonstration presented by the trainers, with alertness, and mindfulness ✓ Ensure the retention of the learned inputs in their long- term memory	The learners will be able to: ✓ Implement the technical skills under the supervision of the trainer ✓ Gain expertise and experience from repeated practice of technical skills ✓ Deploy their achieved expertise, and incurred experience while implementing a technical task ✓ Implement the technical task independently in a flawless ✓ pattern

Functional Competency	Impact upon the understanding process of the learners	Impact upon the application process of the learners
Ability to use digital tools	The learners will be able to comprehend: ✓ The rationale for applying the different digital tools for ensuring conceptual elucidation, and eliciting creative potential ✓ The mechanism of operating the digital tools with ease, and convenience	The learners will be able to: ✓ Apply the digital tools for developing creative projects, under the guidance of the instructors ✓ Apply the digital tools for completing assignments, and developing projects in collaboration with other learners ✓ Apply the digital tools for effective self-learning

Functional Competency	Impact upon the understanding process of the learners	Impact upon the application process of the learners
Ability to identify, and Replenish the learning gap	The learners will be able to: ✓ Perceive their learning gap, and performance-gap, under the guidance of the trainer ✓ Identify the disruptive factors fueling their learning-gap, and performance-gap, under the guidance of the trainer ✓ Conceptualize the strategies that need to be implemented, under the guidance of the trainer.	The learners will be able to: ✓ Implement well-planned strategies for ✓ replenishing/bridging up their learning gaps, and performance gaps under the guidance of the trainer. ✓ Adhere to the preventive strategies that will inhibit the emergence of learning- gaps, and performance - gaps in future

Functional Competency	Impact upon the understanding process of the learners	Impact upon the application process of the learners
Ability to create a conducive learning ambiance	The learners will be able to: ✓ Perceive the supportive features of the conducive learning environment ✓ Identify the cause-effect dynamics between the features of conducive learning environment with the cognitive enrichment & emotive empowerment of the learners	The learners will be able to: ✓ Unleash their hidden potential, and acquire new learning inputs ✓ Emerge as outperformers in the conducive learning environment ✓ Ensure emotive integration with peer learners, and the trainers. ✓ Empathize the problems of the co-learners ✓ Collaborate with peer learners in achieving the common learning goals ✓ Replenish the performance gap of the peer learners

Conclusion

In the present scenario, the Higher Education Teachers should be able to recognize the following linear chain for empowering the learners ;-

Experientia Learning _______________ Competency Development Performance Enhancement

Therefore , the Higher Education Teachers, should acquire Facilitation Techniques for enabling the learners to incur Experiential Learning , to acquire & reinforce competencies and to deliver high quality performance

4

Deployment of Facilitation Tools by the Mentors for developing Psycho-social Competency of the Students

According to ATD (American Association of Talent Development) "Facilitation is the act of engaging participants in creating, discovering, and applying learning insights."

In contrast to the lecture method, which is typically characterized by the "sage on the stage" model of delivering content to the passive audience, Facilitation usually involves a "guide by the side" model that encourages the Facilitators to ask questions, moderate discussion, administer activities, and enable participants to learn.

In Adult Learning, a Facilitator makes judicious utilization of the Participatory Training Methods and Psycho-social Interventions with the following intentions; -

✓ building up a psychological rapport with learners,
✓ reinforcing their confidence level,
✓ triggering achievement motivation within them,
✓ ensuring their proactive participation in the learning process,
✓ engaging them with goal-oriented critical tasks,
✓ developing their analytical acumen.
✓ facilitating them to solve problems by unleashing their creative potential
✓ empowering them to overcome obstacles by unleashing their critical thinking acumen.
✓ facilitating them to achieve previously determined goals through the concerted effort of all the group members

The Mentors can deploy a series of Facilitation tools for enhancing the Psycho-social Competencies of the Students. These psycho-social competencies can enable the learners to deal with the demands and challenges of everyday life.

Some of these Facilitation tools are enumerated below:

A. Motivational Success Stories

Success Stories play an instrumental role in triggering and reinforcing Achievement Motivation within the learners. While composing the Success Story, the Instructional Designer /Facilitator should create the central character/protagonist in such a way, that the learners can identify the central character with themselves. To be precise, the demographic features of the central character/protagonist should be similar to that of the learners.

The learners get motivated by the successful outcome achieved by the Central Character/Protagonist. Eventually, they replicate the outcome-oriented behavior of the Central Character, with the motivational intent of achieving a similar outcome.

Normally the following components are there in a Success Story:
- ✓ A Central Character /Protagonist
- ✓ Achievement Motivation of the Central Character
- ✓ Circumstantial problems that are being encountered by the Central Character
- ✓ Strategies adopted by the Protagonist for overcoming the obstacles /impediments
- ✓ Support from any Mentor /Facilitator
- ✓ Internal Conflicts & External Conflicts
- ✓ Conflict Resolution Strategies adopted by the Protagonist
- ✓ Goal Achievement

Positive Impact of Success Stories upon the Learners
- ✓ The Achievement Motivation of the learners gets enhanced.
- ✓ The learners become more focused on the desired result
- ✓ The psychic fortitude and resilience of the learners get enhanced
- ✓ The learners adopt the goal-oriented behavior of the Central Character through Behavioral Modelling
- ✓ Insightful Stories can foster the analytical acumen of the trainees.
- ✓ Stories can facilitate the trainees in utilizing their existing internal potential judiciously
- ✓ Stories can enable the trainees in deploying the available resources in the external matrix
- ✓ Stories can guide the trainees to solve situational problems through Critical Thinking

B. Role Play:

When the learners are finding it difficult to comprehend a complex topic, then Role-Play is a very effective method of explicating the topic.

The Facilitator/Mentor creates a theme based on the complex topic with some characters that will be interacting among them through relevant dialogues. Then the Facilitator asks some of the learners to enact the role of those characters.

Thus, the incidents are displayed before the other learners through role enactment. By enacting the roles, the Role Players demonstrate complexities in a lucid manner that can be comprehended by the role players themselves as well as the other learners who view the role plays dispassionately

Apart from the elucidation & clarification of the complex thematic issues, Role Plays can play an instrumental role in improving communication skills, developing congenial interpersonal relationships, and fostering collaborative teamwork.

Positive Impact of Role Play upon the learners:-
In Role Play, learning takes place in the following ways; -
✓ Experiential Learning incurred by the actors while enacting the roles
✓ Learning by imitating the behavioral pattern of the Role-Players (Behavioral Modelling)
✓ Learning through reflective observation of the entire Role Play
✓ Learning through analysis of the theme and process of the Role-play and conceptualization drawn from the analysis

C. Case Analysis

Two types of Cases can be given to the learners
✓ Case on Problems
✓ Case on Solution Oriented Strategies

Case Studies on Problems	Case Studies on Solution-oriented Strategic Inputs
✓ At first, the learners are provided with a Problematic Case encapsulating various problems. Then they are asked to explore, analyze and solve the problems that are depicted in the Case.	✓ In this type of Case, the learners are exposed to various problems as well as various strategic action plans that are initiated for solving the problems. ✓ The Facilitator guides the learners to analyze & evaluate the strategies and

✓ The Facilitator guides the learners in analyzing the problems critically, tracing out the causative factors that are triggering the problems, and finally generating creative strategies for solving the problems.	draw inferences regarding the effectiveness of the strategies in solving the problems. The learners are encouraged to detect the pros and cons of the strategic action plans from the perspective of effectiveness
✓ Significant impact on Learners: This type of Case Study will foster both the Critical Thinking & Creative Thinking acumen of the trainees.	✓ Significant Impact on Learners :
	✓ This type of Case Study will build up the Analytical & Evaluative Competency of the learners
✓ It also intensifies the Problem-Solving Skill of the Learners	

D. Situation Analysis & Task Planning

In this intervention, learners are inducted into a simulated situation where they will have to encounter critical problems. Both the situation and the situational problems will be relevant to the subject of learning.

The learners will have to execute an intensive analysis of the situational matrix and the effect of the existing problems as well as the imminent impact of potential problems on the situation. Then they will have to design a Strategic Plan for alleviating the present situational problems and preventing the occurrence of probable situational problems.

It covers the following strategic tasks:
✓ Analysis of the general situation
✓ Analysis of the impact of the problems on the situation
✓ Identification & analysis of the causative factors that are triggering the problems
✓ Planning & developing Stratagems for diluting the causative factors and diminishing the intensity of the manifested problems
✓ Determining Strategies for implementing the Action Plan
✓ Restoring Situational Equilibrium.

Significance:
✓ While carrying out the problem-analysis and generating strategic solutions, many cognitive competencies of the learners like Critical thinking and Problem-Solving will get manifested.
✓ Since the learners are made a part of the situation, the empathy of the learners toward the people suffering from problems gets enhanced
✓ Situational Analysis & Planning Exercise plays an important role in enhancing the motivation, engagement, and empowerment of the learners

E. Situation Driven Role Enactmernt

✓ Situation-Driven Role Enactment is a participatory learning methodology that elicits creative potential, analytical competency, decision-making power, and problem-solving capacity from the learners.
✓ It is based on the concept of Forum Theatre developed by Augusto Boal the great dramatist, play-writer, and social change-maker of Brazil.
✓ In this methodology, Role-Play is designed with exploitation, conflict, and problems in thematic components. One group of learners is encouraged by the Facilitator to enact the different roles. The other group of learners is advised by the Facilitator to observe the Role -Play with deep contemplation
✓ During the execution of the Role Play, when a situation reflects the optimum level of exploitation and oppression, then the Facilitator encourages the Observers to enact the role of supportive and benevolent characters.
✓ Eventually, they are encouraged by the Facilitator to design instrumental strategies instantly that can mitigate the connivance of the exploitative Role Players and dilute exploitation to a great extent.
✓ Thus, the observers are enacting roles spontaneously and instantly on the basis of institutional crisis. Situational crisis and exigency are the factors that drive the enactment of benevolent roles.

This method facilitates the learners in the following ways; -
○ It enhances the creativity of the learners
○ It reinforces the analytical acumen of the learners
○ It builds up the crisis-management capacity of the learners
○ It enhances the empathetic sensitivity of the learners

F. Scaffolding :

Scaffolding: The term Scaffolding was initiated by **Jerome Bruner**.

In this technique, the Facilitator extends comprehensive guidance and hand-holding support to a learner, when the learner is executing a newly learned task.

According to Jerome Bruner, if a learner is provided with active guidance and hand-holding support (Scaffolding) by an Expert during the implementation of a newly learned task, then his/her performance will be much better than the performance delivered by the learner without the hand-holding support (Scaffolding) from an expert.

	Interventions	Results
A.	The Facilitator provides active guidance and hand-holding support to a novice learner when he is performing a newly learned task	Learner delivers significantly higher level of Performance (from both qualitative and quantitative perspectives
B,	The facilitator remains passive without extending support to the novice learner when the latter is performing a newly learned task	Learner delivers comparatively, Lower level of Performance (from both qualitative and quantitative perspectives)

G. Positive Reinforcement

When a learner is manifesting a desired behavior or delivering noteworthy performance in the classroom, then the Educator /Facilitator appreciates or provides appreciation /acknowledgment/non-financial rewards to the learners for every manifestation of the desired behavior.

Here appreciation/acknowledgment and rewards from the Facilitator are to be considered as the Reinforcing Stimuli for encouraging the learners in ensuring repetition of the desired behavior or performance.

Eventually, it will be found that the frequency of the desired behavior/performance (pertaining to learning) will get enhanced considerably.

Significance:

- o This technique enhances the achievement motivation of the learners
- o This technique elevates the self-confidence and self-esteem of the learners
- o This technique is instrumental in engineering behavioral change in the learner
- o This technique is capable of transforming a desired behavior (pertaining to learning) into a sustainable habit

H. Behavioral Modelling :

The Mentor/Facilitator highlights the success of the best performer in the learning session and appreciates his/her success. Then he categorically enumerates the outcome-oriented behavioral attributes of the best performer that are the causative factors behind his/her success

Thus, the Facilitator indirectly motivates the other learners to consider the best performer as Role model and to replicate the positive behavioral attributes of the best performer that are causally linked to his success.

The learners perceive that if they replicate the outcome-oriented behaviour of the best performer then they will also receive appreciation from the Facilitator.

As a result, the learners initiate **Behavioral Modelling** (viz. replication of the outcome-oriented behaviour of the best performer)

In this way an Educator /Facilitator can enhance the achievement motivation of the average performers, encourage them to execute Behavioral Modelling of the outcome-oriented behaviour of the best performer, and can steer them towards desired success

N.B. **This method is based on Social Learning Theory of Albert Bandura**

Significance:
- o This technique enhances the Achievement Motivation of the learners
- o This technique builds up a result-focused attitude within the learners
- o This technique crystallizes success -orientation within the learners

I. Cognitive Apprenticeship Model

Cognitive Apprenticeship Model: Through this technique, a Facilitator guides the learners to implement a newly learned skill-based task. This technique encapsulates six steps. Each step is driven by a valued intent.
- ✓ **Modelling:** The Facilitator demonstrates a skill-based task before the learners
- ✓ **Coaching:** The Facilitator encourages the learners to implement the demonstrated task independently without the support of the facilitator. After observing the performance of the learners, the Facilitator specifies the AOI viz. areas where improvement is required

- ✓ **Scaffolding:** The Facilitator provides active support and guidance to the learners during the implementation of the newly learned task
- ✓ **Articulation**: The Facilitator encourages the learners to portray /illustrate the entire process of implementing the task under the guidance of the Facilitator
- ✓ **Reflection:** The Facilitator motivates the learners to compare their demonstration with the demonstration of the Facilitator
- ✓ **Exploration:** The Facilitator inspires the learners to explore new strategies for enhancing the quality of their demonstration.

Significance:
- ✓ This technique enables the learners in implementing newly learned skill
- ✓ This technique gradually builds up the functional competencies and self-confidence of the learners
- ✓ This technique fosters analytical acumen and creative potential of the learners

J. Appreciative Inquiry

Appreciative Inquiry is a strength-focused intervention that aims at identifying the core strength and competence prevailing/existing within the learners. The Facilitator utilizes this intervention, especially for the learners who are not aware of their core competence.

In this technique, the Facilitator asks encouraging questions with the aim of tracing out the achievements of the learners in the recent past. Once the learner reveals his/her achievement, the Facilitator can analyze the performance and ascertain the causative competency factors, embedded within the learners, that have fueled the recent achievement. Subsequently, the Facilitator makes a concerted effort to enable the learners in utilizing their identified competencies

There are four steps in Appreciative Inquiry. Each step is driven by a distinct valued intent; -
- ✓ **Discovery Phase**: Through penetrating questions, the Facilitator tries to trace out the past achievements as well as the core competencies of the learners that are pent up within them

✓ **Dream Phase**: In this stage, the learners are encouraged by the Facilitator to envision a bright and prosperous future that can be created by judicious utilization of the core strength /competence of the learners
✓ **Design Phase**: The Facilitator inspires the learners to design a Strategic Action Plan utilizing their core strengths & competence so that they can reach their envisioned future
✓ **Deploy Phase**: The Facilitator motivates the learners to deploy their strength /competence and reach the envisioned future

Significance : Through this technique,Mentors can facilitate the learners in the following ways ;-

❖ The learners will get sensitized regarding their core competencies
❖ The learners will envision a futuristic developmental goal that can be achieved by the judicious utilization of the core competencies of the learners
❖ The learners will be able to follow goal-oriented strategic action plan designed by the Mentors .
❖ The learners will continually get enriched by the Motivational Inputs , Guided instructions and the Hand-holding Support of the learners

K. Cognitive Restructuring

This Facilitation technique is applied when the cognitive system of the learners is reflecting distortions, irrationality and deviation from the logical rationale.

When the Facilitator perceives that the learner is suffering from cognitive distortions and irrationality, then at first he tries to trace out causative factors/reasons behind such distortions and irrationality.

Then the Facilitator explains the learner about the negative result chain that is existing within his cognition

Negative Cognitive-Behavioral Result Chain

Cognitive Distortions	Negative Behaviour	Negative Performance	Negative Outcome

The Facilitator enables the learners in identifying, comprehending and validating the negative result chain existing within him. He also encourages the learner to replace the Negative Cognitive-Behavioral Result Chain with an alternative Positive Cognitive Behavioral Result Chain presented by him.

Positive Result Chain

Logically Governed Thought Process	Positive Behaviour	Positive Performance	Positive Outcome

After that the Facilitator guides the learner to execute comparative analysis between the two Result Chains and facilitates the learner to identify and comprehend the favourable attributes of the Positive Result Chain and the detrimental attributes of the Negative Result Chain embedded within his cognition

After that the learner gradually makes a shift from the Negative Result Chain to the Positive Result Chain

This shift is the outcome of the Cognitive Restructuring engineered by the Facilitator.

Design Thinking :

This is an advanced Facilitation Technique. Design Thinking is the only strategic methodology in the global arena that initiates with Empathy and ends with Empathy It facilitates the learners in eliciting their pent up creativity and analytical flair.

There are six steps in Design Thinking

Fi	Empathy	The Facilitator/Mentor gets the learners exposed to a group of problem-stricken beneficiaries and encouraged them to identify the problems of these people with empathetic outlook and approach
	Problem Definition	At this stage the learners will collate all the discrete problems and give a concrete definition to the collated problem
T	Ideation	At this stage , the Facilitator/Mentor inspires the learners to float a bunch of creative ideas aimed at problem solving
F	Prototype Develoipment	At this stage , the Facilitator guides the learners to select the most cost-effective and viable solution and create a tangible prototype of the solution

| Fi | Testing | At this stage, the prototype is presented to a sample of the problem stricken beneficiaries for testing. The feedback /response of the beneficiaries are meticulously recorded |
| S | Re-Engineering | Based on the response shared by the beneficiaries regarding the prototype , the Facilitator guides the learners in Re-engineering the prototype and shaping the final product or service |

Significance :
- o Design Thinking elicits the creative potential of the learners
- o Design Thinking intensifies the creativity of the learners
- o Design thinking crystallizes empathetic sensitivity to the problem-stricken people
- o Design Thinking is an instrumental intervention for enhancing cognitive proficiency and emotive intensity

L. Mind Mapping

In this developmental intervention, the Facilitator/Mentor at first presents a significant theme (highly relevant to the learning content) to the learners. He suggested the learners to consider this significant theme as the Central Concept.

Then the learners are encouraged to analyze the Central Concept and split it into different thematic components. Eventually, each thematic component is segregated into different sub-components

Then the Facilitator/Mentor asks the learners to find out the relationship connections or associations among the different segregated components and sub-components of the central theme.

Then the learners are encouraged to find out the different beneficial features of each of the thematic components and identify the beneficial impact created by each beneficial feature upon the diversified target audience

In this way, different offshoots get created from each of the sub-components of the central concept.

Significance:
- o This technique fosters divergent thinking within the learners
- o This technique enhances the analytical capacity of the learners

M. Force-Field Analysis

This is an advanced Facilitation technique based on the Force Field Analysis theory by Kurt Lewin

In this Facilitation technique, the Facilitator places the learners in simulated realistic situations where there are many factors.

Firstly, the Facilitator encourages the Learner to determine a goal within the situational framework

After the completion of Goal determination , the Facilitator inspires the learner to analyze the situational framework critically and to trace out the following factors ;-

- o Situational Drivers (these are the supporting factors that are facilitating the learner in enhancing his/her momentum toward the goal and in achieving the previously determined goal)
- o Situational Inhibitors (these are the detrimental factors that are diminishing the goal-oriented momentum of the learner and restricting the learner in achieving the previously determined goal)

Examples of Situational Drivers :-
- o Coaches
- o Mentors
- o Friends & Sympathizers
- o Opinion Builders in the Situational Framework who will influence others in emanating positive support toward the goal –oriented initiative of the learner

Examples of Situational Inhibitors :-
- o Competitors
- o Rivals
- o Individuals having conflicting –dynamics with the learner

---

Finally, the Facilitator guides the learner in designing strategic interventions for intensifying the Situational Drivers and strategic interventions for diluting the Situational Inhibitors

Significance: This strategic intervention is highly instrumental for fostering cognitive competencies like Critical Thinking, Creative Thinking, Problem Solving , and Decision Making

N. Inquiry-based Facilitation

In this method, the Facilitator floats multifarious open-ended queries relevant to the topic of learning and encourage the learners to ventilate their independent and unbiased views and opinion regarding the aforementioned floated queries. The Facilitator will also inspire the learners to identify the logical rationale behind their views and opinions

Significance:
- This intervention will enhance the analytical acumen of the learners
- This intervention will expand the creative potential and the imaginative horizon of the learners
- This intervention will foster meta-cognitive competency among the learners
- This intervention will facilitate the learners to integrate their existing knowledge with the novel inputs acquired through experiential learning

N.B. What is meta-cognition?

Meta-cognition is the thought which is influencing another thought or inducing another action. It can be deemed as the cognitive rationale which is determining a chain of thoughts or a complex thought- process.

Learners with a high level of meta-cognitive competency are capable of tracing out the core cognitive rationale which is the root cause of the core causative factor behind a prolonged and critical thought-chain

O. Quality Circle & Participatory Planning

The Facilitator divides the learners into different groups and allocates an Assignment to each group.

The members of each group execute a collective analysis of the assignment and thereafter execute collaborative planning regarding the strategy and process of completing the assignment.

Then the group members encourage each of the members in the group to contribute creative ideas for enriching the process of completing the assignment and add value to the assignment for ensuring its qualitative excellence

During process implementation, the group members make a collective effort for monitoring the jointly determined process and preventing any deviation from the determined process

Significance:
  o This technique fosters collaboration among the learners
  o This technique boosts the creative potential of the learners
  o This technique builds up quality consciousness among the learners
  o This technique makes the learners equipped with the skill of process -
    monitoring and process management

P. Facilitation through Active Listening & Paraphrasing:

Facilitation is a dialogue-driven intervention, where the Facilitator continually motivates the learners to narrate the inputs learned during the process of facilitation.

When the learners continue to narrate their learned inputs, the Facilitator actively listens to the narration of the learners. **Active Listening** makes it easy for the Facilitator to analyze and evaluate the narration of the learners.

After the completion of the narration of the learners, the Facilitator repeats the essence of the narration of the learners but in a more polished, refined, and sophisticated language. He also prunes the irrelevant part of the learners' narration, replenishes the gaps, and adds value to it. This is termed as **Paraphrasing**

❖ Thus, after the completion of Paraphrasing, the learners can understand which of the topics they missed out and the points which were irrelevant. The learners learn from the paraphrased statements.
❖ The learners also feel confident, when they find that the Facilitator is repeating the essence of his narration or idea before others, removing the irrelevant parts.
❖ It also gives pleasure to the learners when they understand that the Educator/Facilitator was listening to their narration actively, before paraphrasing

Significance:
  o Paraphrasing instills confidence within the learners
  o Paraphrasing facilitates the learners to identify their learning gaps and bridge them accordingly

5

Deployment of Goal Oriented Analytical & Strategic Planning Tools by Mentors for developing Result -Focused Attitude of the Students

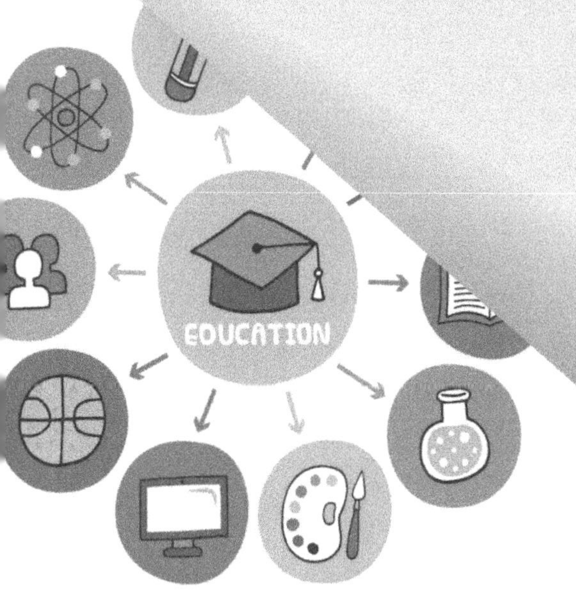

The Mentors shepherd the learners towards previously determined goals . They also develop a Result -Oriented Approach within the learners

An effort has been made by us to specify and clarify some **Goal Oriented Planning Tools** that can be judiciously deployed by the Mentors for steering the learners toward their desired outcome

A. ORACLE MODEL

O	OBJECTIVE & EXPECTED OUTCOME	✓ What is the objective of a student in the learning journey? ✓ What is the outcome that he is expecting after the completion of his learning journey?
R	REAL ISSUE	✓ What are the underlying issues that are shaping the objective and the expected outcome? ✓ Are the underlying issues realistic and concrete?
A	ALTERNATIVES	✓ What are the alternative strategies that can be applied for facilitating the students to achieve ✓ their expected outcome?
C	CREATIVE IDEAS	✓ How to add value to the existing strategies? ✓ How is it possible to develop nprecedented strategies that can transfer the objectives into tangible outcome?
L	LIKELIHOOD OF SUCCESS	✓ Evaluating the viability and likelihood of ✓ strategies in a 1-10 point scale
E	EXECUTE	✓ What is the Strategy? ✓ Who will be involved for implementing the strategy ✓ Who will provide support to implementing entities? ✓ How will the strategy get implemented in a step by step manner?

B. GROW MODEL

Goal	Facilitating the students to determine their goal in a learning /educational project
Reality	Facilitating the student to appraise his present status with specification of the available resources
Options	Facilitating the students to identify the alternative ptions/alternative strategies to reach their previously determined goal
Will	Facilitating the students to express their will viz. how they are planning to determine the pathway through which they will reach the goal

C. OSKAR Model:
✓ Outcome: Define the desired outcome or goal.
✓ Scaling: Assess the current situation and identify any gaps.
✓ Know-how: Brainstorm and identify potential strategies and solutions.
✓ Action: Develop an action plan with specific steps and timelines.
✓ Review: Evaluate progress and make necessary adjustments.

D. CLEAR Model:
✓ C: Contracting: Establish clear goals and expectations for the coaching relationship.
✓ L: Listening: Actively listen to the learners' perspective and concerns.
✓ E: Exploring: Explore the learners' situation and identify potential solutions.
✓ A: Action: Develop an action plan with specific steps and timelines.
✓ R: Review: Evaluate progress and make necessary adjustments.

E. ACHIEVE Model:
✓ Assess: Assess the current situation and identify the learners' strengths and weaknesses.
✓ Collaborate: Work with the learners to set goals and objectives.
✓ Hone Goals: Refine goals and objectives to ensure they are SMART (Specific, Measurable, Achievable, Relevant, and Time-bound).
✓ Implement Actions: Develop an action plan with specific steps and timelines.
✓ Evaluate: Evaluate progress and make necessary adjustments.

F. GOAL ANALYSIS

The Mentor analyses the Goal of the Students through the following framework

✓ What is the goal of the student?
✓ Why does the student want to achieve the Goal?
✓ What are the requisite resources to achieve the Goal?
✓ What is the time frame within which the goal has to be achieved?
✓ What will be the significant Milestones?
✓ Which factors should be considered as the Critical Success Factors for Goal achievement?
✓ What should be the Key Performance Indicator at every Milestone ?
✓ How can we track the process?
✓ What should be the strategy of there is any deviation from the right path?
✓ What should be the strategic check points for preventing further deviations

Obstacle Analysis

✓ This is an extremely crucial exercise of strategic planning which is essential in the learning journey of a student

✓ In many instances the student finds that despite his sustained effort as well as the existence of requisite resource, he is not being able to achieve his goal.

✓ This is due to various internal inhibitors within the students as well as circumstantial obstacles that are impeding their momentum in the learning journey and preventing them to achieve the desired learning goal.

✓ Under such circumstances the Facilitator will enable the students to critically analyze their internal inhibitors as well as their circumstantial obstacles and facilitate the students to develop the strategy for removal of such obstacles or inhibitors.

✓ How the appropriate strategies can be selected and implemented for removal of the external obstacles?
✓ How the External blocks are impeding the progression of the students?
✓ What is the root cause of such external blocks?
✓ What are the external blocks?
✓ What is the mental status of the students when they are getting blocked from achieving the desired outcome ?
✓ How would the Facilitator motivate students to remove the blocks?
✓ What are the alternative strategies that can be framed to remove the blocks?
✓ What are the resources within the students for implementing each of the alternative strategies for removing the block?
✓ What are the additional resources that the Facilitator would like to leverage for implementing each of the alternative strategies for removing the block?
✓ What are the additional resources that the Facilitator would like to leverage for implementing each of the alternative strategies for removing the block?   ✓ How the alternative strategies can be rated in terms of feasibility, time and potential to achieve the goal?   ✓ Out of the different alternative strategies, how the most appropriate   ✓ strategies can be selected and implemented for removal of the external obstacles?

(II) Internal Obstacle Analysis

✓ What are the psychic factors within the students that are inhibiting their journey towards goal?
✓ How these inhibiting factors have emerged within them?
✓ What are the manifested behaviors associated with their internal inhibition?
✓ What emotion/feelings are getting triggered due the inhibition within the students?
✓ Why are the students not being able to overcome the psychological inhibitor?
✓ Have they ever tried to overcome such inhibitions?
✓ What were their past strategies and why were they non-functional ?
✓ How many alternative strategies can they develop to overcome psychological inhibitors?
✓ Comparative analysis of the Alternatives and &selection of the most feasible one
✓ Implementation of the most appropriate/feasible strategy for removing the Internal Inhibitors

Strategic Interventions to be deployed by Mentors for fostering different categories of knowledge and enhancing cognitive competency from one level to another level of Cognitive Taxonomy

According to D.R Krathwohl , there are four categories of knowledge

Structure of Knowledge dimension by D.R Krathwohl

1	Factual Knowledge	✓ The basic elements that students must know to be acquainted with a discipline or solve problems in it. ○ Aa. Knowledge of terminology ○ Ab. Knowledge of specific details and element
2	Conceptual knowledge	✓ The interrelationships among the basic elements within a larger structure that enable them to function together. ○ Ba. Knowledge of classifications and categories ○ Bb. Knowledge of principles and generalizations ○ Bc. Knowledge of theories, models, and structures
3	Procedural Knowledge	✓ How to do something; methods of inquiry, and criteria for using skills, algorithms, techniques, and methods. ○ Ca. Knowledge of subject-specific skills and algorithms ○ Cb. Knowledge of subject-specific techniques and methods ○ Cc. Knowledge of criteria for determining when to use appropriate procedures
4	Metacognitive Knowledge	✓ Knowledge of cognition in general as well as awareness and knowledge of one's cognition. ○ Da. Strategic knowledge ○ Db. Knowledge about cognitive tasks, including appropriate contextual and conditional knowledge ○ Dc. Self-knowledge

Detailed Descriptions

Factual Knowledge

✓ Factual Knowledge is the knowledge that is basic to specific disciplines. This dimension refers to essential facts, terminology, details, or elements that the learners must know or be familiar with, to understand a discipline or solve a problem in it. ✓ Example: A learner in the Beauty & Wellness sector is well aware of certain specific indigenous Beauty Products and their application for ensuring the benefit of the customers

Conceptual Knowledge

Conceptual Knowledge is knowledge of classifications, principles, generalizations, theories, models, or structures pertinent to a particular disciplinary area.

- o **Example**: A Learner in the Beauty & Wellness Sector is capable of classifying indigenous Beauty Products according to their specific, detailed, and minute functional utilities. She has a deep cognitive clarity regarding the composition of beauty products, the utility of each of the ingredients, the resultant reaction of the bio-chemical combination of one ingredient with another ingredient, the pH value of each ingredient, and the pH value of the consolidated end-product. , the pattern of storage and usage of each beauty product, and the effect of each product on human health

Procedural Knowledge

Procedural Knowledge refers to information or knowledge that helps learners to do something specific to a discipline, subject, or area of study. It also refers to methods of inquiry, very specific or finite skills, algorithms, techniques, and particular methodologies.

- o **Example**: A learner in the Beauty & Wellness Sector is capable of procuring raw materials from appropriate sources, washing them with an appropriate cleansing agent, getting them dried, crushing them into powdered form blending them in a judicious concentration and finally developing comprehensive indigenous beauty products. Then she can get the end products packed and branded meticulously, and store them in a suitable location.

Metacognitive Knowledge

Metacognitive Knowledge: It is strategic or reflective knowledge about how to administer cognitive strategies for solving problems, the intricacies of cognitive tasks to be performed (including contextual and conditional knowledge), and the knowledge of self.

Example: A Learner in the Beauty and Wellness Sector Skill Council is well aware of the following;

- o her cognitive capability in conducting research regarding the beneficial exclusivity of indigenous beauty products, and writing a comprehensive document on the research findings

<table>
<tr><td colspan="2">

- o the detailed terms and conditions of developing the research-driven document
- o the strategies that are to be adopted for conducting the primary research, executing the process -documentation, and writing the comprehensive report on the research findings with the process -analysis

</td></tr>
</table>

Role of Facilitation techniques, to be adopted by Mentors, in enhancing the intensity of different categories of knowledge

Facilitation Techniques for Enhancing the Intensity of Factual Knowledge	✓ **Story Telling:** A story having relevance to the curriculum should be narrated in lucid language avoiding any complexity of jargon. This methodology can make the learners acquainted with factual details ✓ **Paraphrasing:** After the learners communicate their factual knowledge, the Facilitator should paraphrase using his own words with greater sophistication. This methodology facilitates the learners to achieve a deeper understanding of the factual details ✓ **Parenthesis:** Every critical jargon should be accompanied by detailed elaboration so that the learners find it easy to acquire factual knowledge. ✓ **Metaphors & Analogies:** If the theoretical factual elements are accompanied by appropriate practical examples that are known to the learners, then it becomes easier for the learners to acquire factual knowledge
Facilitation Techniques for Enhancing the Intensity of Conceptual Knowledge	✓ **Affinity Diagram:** The learners are given a bunch of concepts. Then they are asked to identify similar concepts and put all the similar concepts in a specific category. Thus, ultimately the learners will have to construct a certain number of categories and each category should include similar concepts having an affinity

	✓ **Venn Diagram:** Learners are asked to execute comparative analysis among a bunch of concepts and encouraged to trace out the common and uncommon features among these concepts ✓ **Mind Mapping:** A central concept is given to the learner. Eventually, the learners are asked to develop as many categories and associations as possible, that are relevant to the central concept
Facilitation Techniques for Enhancing the Intensity of Procedural Knowledge	✓ **Structured Simulations:** The learners will have to participate in Structured Simulations which reflect the same process of a real situation. While enacting specific roles in the Structured Simulation and replicating the process followed in realistic situations, the learners will gain procedural knowledge. ✓ **Scaffolding:** After the learners acquire a new skill, they are encouraged by the Facilitator to implement the new skill practically. During the practical implementation of the newly acquired skill, the learners are provided with complete handholding support and holistic guidance. Thus, due to the comprehensive handholding support of the Facilitator, the learners gain procedural knowledge, during the practical implementation of acquired skills.
Facilitation Techniques for Enhancing the Intensity of the three components of Metacognitive Knowledge	**Inquiry-Based Facilitation & Discovery Learning:** Based on the theory of Jerome Bruner, the Facilitator floats gentle queries and encourages the learners to frame relevant replies to the queries. o The conducive queries of the Facilitator inspire the learners to be more introspective. The learners try to trace out the core cognitive rationale which is

	inducing their thoughts and actions. The logical flair of the learners gets enhanced. With greater logical and analytical acumen, the learners can monitor and evaluate their cognitive functions. Thus, the learners gain **self-knowledge** ○ When the queries of the Facilitator are related to certain specific tasks, then the learners try to present their feedback after a critical analysis of the task. This practice builds up the analytical capacity of the learners and at the same time, the **task knowledge** of the learners gets enhanced. Thus, it can be inferred that **Inquiry-Based Facilitation & Discovery Learning** play an instrumental role in facilitating the learners in achieving conceptual clarity regarding the task to be performed ○ Inquiry Based Facilitation and cognitive probing are instrumental in facilitating the learners to introspect and ex[press their latent creative potential. By judicious deployment of their creative prowess, the learners develop strategies for implementing their task as well as for alleviating the operational problems about task implementation. Thus, it can be inferred that Inquiry-Based Facilitation and cognitive probing are capable of eliciting the pent-up creative flair of the learners and enhancing their **strategic knowledge** Thus, to conclude it can be rationally opined that the Inquiry-Based Facilitation and Discovery Learning Theory of **Jerome Bruner** are instrumental in fostering the three components of Metacognitive Knowledge viz. Self-Knowledge, Task knowledge, and Strategic knowledge

Inductive Strategic Interventions deployed by the Mentors for upgrading Cognitive Competencies of different categories of learners: -

Category 1:

Identified Entry Behavior	Through Empathetic Interaction with the learners, it has been identified by the Facilitator that the learners can remember a concept but are not capable of comprehending the concept.
Learning Objectives determined	To facilitate the learners in comprehending the concept
Inductive Pedagogy driven Strategic Interventions	o The learners will be encouraged to observe and understand some practical incidents. o The learners deeply reflect on the practical incidents and develop a concept o Eventually, the learners can integrate the concepts crystallized through reflection on Practical incidents with the existing knowledge of the learners o Thus, an association is established between the new theoretical inputs with the existing concepts of the learners, that they have developed through deep reflection on practical incidents
Expected Outcome	It is expected that the learners will be capable of comprehending the theoretical concept.

Category 2:

Identified Entry Behavior	Through Empathetic Interaction with the learners, it has been identified by the Facilitator that the learners can comprehend a concept but are not capable of applying the essence of it in a practical situation.
Learning Objectives determined	To facilitate the learners in applying the concept in a practical situation
Inductive Pedagogy Driven Strategic	✓ Getting the learners exposed to practical situations and motivating them to translate the concept into practice ✓ Facilitating the learners in crystallizing self-confidence for applying the concept with composure

Interventions	✓ Providing guided instructions and handholding support to the learners, when they are applying the concept practically ✓ Appreciating and acknowledging the positivity and the efforts of the learners, when they are engaged in practical application ✓ Facilitating the learners to get practical experiences documented ✓ Encouraging the learners to reflect on each of the documented experiences while executing the task practically ✓ Facilitating the process of conceptualization viz. development of new concepts based on reflection on experiences ✓ Encouraging the learners to integrate their experientially acquired concepts with their existing theoretical understanding
Expected Outcome	It is expected that the learners will be able to apply the concept into practice, with precision and confidence.

Category 3:

Identified Entry Behavior	Through Empathetic Interaction with the learners, it has been identified by the Facilitator that the Learners can apply the concept but can't analyze it.
Learning Objectives determined	To facilitate the learners in developing analytical competency
Inductive Pedagogy Driven Strategic Interventions	First Intervention: ✓ Getting the learners exposed to five different theories and models ✓ Subsequently, the learners will be motivated to trace out the common features and the uncommon features among the different theories and models ✓ Finally, the learners will be asked to place the common features in one category and the uncommon features in another category Second Intervention: ✓ The learners are provided with an Integrated Learning System

	✓ The learners are encouraged to analyze the Integrated Learning System and trace out the different learning styles embedded in the Integrated Learning System ✓ The learners are inspired to trace out their preferred learning style
Expected Outcome	It is expected that the aforementioned inductive interventions will be effective enough to develop analytical competency in the learners.

Category 4:

Identified Entry Behavior	Through Empathetic Interaction with the learners, it has been identified by the Facilitator that the learners can analyze a concept but are not capable of evaluating it.
Learning Objectives determined	To facilitate the learners in developing evaluative competency within them
Inductive Pedagogy Driven Strategic Interventions	**First Intervention** ✓ The learners are encouraged to administer three different vocational skills among rural youth through a uniform Digital Learning Solution. ✓ Each rural youth was equipped with three vocational skills and became competent enough to implement the three vocational skills. ✓ After a considerable period, the learners are asked to evaluate the socioeconomic status of the trained rural youth, with the intent of finding out which one of the three vocational skills has been most instrumental in generating maximum livelihood and contributing toward the socio-economic empowerment of the rural youth.
	Second Intervention: ✓ The learners are provided with a reliable and valid Standard of Operations (SOP) ✓ Then the learners are exposed to five different application maneuvers, executed by five individuals

	✓ Finally, the learners are encouraged to evaluate each application maneuver with the Standard of Operation (SOP) and rate each application maneuver on a rating scale
Expected Outcome	It is expected that the learners will be capable of administering evaluative competency.

Category 5:

Identified Entry Behavior	Through Empathetic Interaction with the learners, it has been identified by the Facilitator that the learners can evaluate a concept but are not capable of creating innovative conceptual paradigms or innovative models.
Learning Objectives determined	To facilitate the learners in developing the competency of Creative Thinking
Inductive Pedagogy Driven Strategic Interventions	First Intervention: ✓ The learners are exposed to a problem faced by some people ✓ The learners are encouraged to generate innovative ideas for solving the problem ✓ The learners are inspired to execute a comparative analysis of the generated ideas and to select the most cost-effective strategic solution from the perspective of the beneficiaries (viz. the people for whom the learners are developing creative solutions) ✓ The learners are motivated to draw the selected solution in the form of a Flowchart or Mind Mapping template and logically establish how the selected strategic solution will be instrumental in alleviating the problems of the learners
	Second Intervention: The learners are provided with an app for "Gamified Learning" that can trigger entertainment among the students of primary school. Now the learners are encouraged to write their ideas for ▪ Substituting the existing methodology of learning with another effective learning methodology

	<ul><li>Combining the existing learning methodology with any other congruent Learning methodology so that the combined learning methodology becomes more conducive for the learners</li><li>Adjusting the existing learning methodology to make it conducive and convenient for the students of many primary schools irrespective of their demographic and cognitive heterogeneity</li><li>Modifying the existing learning methodology according to the revised curriculum of primary schools</li><li>Putting to other Uses: Reengineering the existing Learning Methodology for cognitive development as well as for developing the emotional intelligence of the learners</li><li>Eliminating the superfluity of the learning methodology to make it more entertaining and thrilling</li><li>Reversing the learning methodology to make it appropriate for the students of High School who have greater cognitive maturity</li></ul>
Expected Outcome	It is expected that the learners will be able to develop Creative Competency.

***

7

Inclusion & Psychological Safety

It is the responsibility of the Mentor to ensure the Inclusion and equality of all the students in the academic institutions who are marked by geographic and demographic heterogeneity.

The Mentors should build up a culture of Inclusion and equality in the Institutions.

Each of the students will perceive the value of inclusion and equality , when he/she will find that

- ✓ There is no Gender Bias in the Institution. Students are not being discriminated on the basis of gender
- ✓ He/she is not getting alienated due to the communication pattern (viz. Communication in local dialect)
- ✓ He/she is not being isolated due to economic background
- ✓ He/she is not getting alienated due to caste/creed/religion
- ✓ He/she is not getting ignored due to underperformance
- ✓ He/She is having equal access to all the learning materials like other students
- ✓ He/she is getting Positive Reinforcement from the Teachers like the other students
- ✓ He/she has equal right to participate in all the academic or recreational events in the Institution like other students
- ✓ He /she is being integrated in the Group Discussion Process led by the Faculty Members or Peer Educators .
- ✓ He /she is not becoming the victim of Subjective Bias of any Faculty Member or Administrative Functionary in the Institution .
- ✓ He/she has got the right to represent the Institution in any Social Platform.

Psychological Safety

Dr. Amy C. Edmondson is often credited with coining the term "psychological safety"—and, more particularly, framing the concept in workplace terms. In 1999, Edmondson **defined ps**ychological safety in the workplace as "the belief that one will not be punished or humiliated for speaking up with ideas, questions, concerns, or mistakes, and that the team is safe for interpersonal risk taking."

The concept of Psychological Safety is highly relevant in Higher Education institutions Ideally in an ambiance marked by psychological safety,the students are encouraged to express their views and opinions with transparency , candor and this much of confidence regarding the proposition /institutional culture , that they will never get chastised , ,humiliated and rebuked , after delivering his own viewpoints.

To ensure the psychological safety of each of the students the Mentors should take the following controlling measures ;-

- ✓ A student should never be criticized for his/her appearance and attire
- ✓ A student should not get humiliated due to her caste/creed/religion
- ✓ A student should not be criticized publicly due to under performance
- ✓ A student should not be criticized by a teacher for inappropriate answer to any question . Rather , the teacher should adopt paraphrasing strategy for facilitating the student to perceive his/her gaps
- ✓ A student should not receive spiteful comments from any Academic or Administrative Functionary in the Institution
- ✓ A mediocre student should not be compared with a meritorious student for highlighting their proficiency-gap.
- ✓ A student should always be encouraged by Motivational Inputs and Positive Reinforcement of every small success.
- ✓ A student should be given the opportunity to participate in the Learning Process
- ✓ Ease and comfort of every student should be ensured while expressing his/her personal thoughts and opinions with candor and transparency.
- ✓ The Mentors should have trauma healing capacity . They should provide comprehensive support to a student if he/she becomes the victim of trauma within the institution
- ✓ Every student should be protected from Sexual Harassment within the Institution .

Well Being

According to World Health organization , Well-being is a positive state experienced by individuals and societies. Similar to health, it is a resource for daily life and is determined by social, economic and environmental conditions. Well-being encompasses quality of life and the ability of people and societies to contribute to the world with a sense of meaning and purpose. Focusing on well-being supports the tracking of the equitable distribution of resources, overall thriving and sustainability.

According McPherson et al. (2019) there are five basic strategies for ensuring well being of the learners

- ✓ Offer opportunities to discuss any concerns with learners prior to a group work activity – especially if this is assessed. Try not to make assumptions based on any disclosed disability and treat each learner as an individual with their own needs.
- ✓ Be clear on the purpose of the activity and be prepared to offer an alternative if a learner cannot participate. It might be that you can offer a dedicated role within the group which is less exposing but still allows for their participation.
- ✓ Allow extra time for reading and thinking around the task – this will help learners with specific conditions, such as dyslexia or dyspraxia, as well as those who may experience 'brain fog' due to medications, etc.
- ✓ Allow learners to choose from a range of communication types – this could include verbal, written or, in online environments, the use of text boxes and polls.
- ✓ Acknowledge success once an activity has finished – this can be about the process of the activity as much as the output of it.

Dr. Martin Seligman has structured a Model for Well-Being with 5 components;
- ✓ Positive emotion
- ✓ Engagement
- ✓ Relationship
- ✓ Meaning of Life
- ✓ Accomplishment

It can be logically inferred that Well -Being of the Learners is the outcome of Psychosocial Mentoring executed by the Higher Education Teachers.

Learners experiencing well being will manifest the following characteristic features

Positive Emotion	The learners are able to emanate positive emotions like happiness , positive approach , compassion , trust, empathy.
Engagement	The learners get engaged with their preferred activities
Relationship	The learners are being able to maintain reciprocally supportive relationship with others
Meaning of Life	The learners can identify the purpose of their life and very eager to make their lives meaningful.
Accomplishment	The learners are being able to achieve their tasks with precision and meticulousness.

In this context , it is relevant and logical to draw the reference of Carl Roger's Theory of humanistic learning which fosters psychological safety and well being

According to Carl Rogers, there are three essential pre-requisites for orchestrating Adult Learning:

- o **Realness in the Facilitator of Learning**: Rogers affirms that this is the most crucial and needed quality. If the teacher functions as a real person, reflecting his/her personal attributes, and if he/she crystallizes a "personal" relationship with the learner, without a facade, then the teacher will be significantly more effective in providing a congenial environment that is conducive to optimal learning.
- o **Prizing, acceptance, and trust:** When a teacher executes appropriate activities to reflect the actual meaning of "prizing," then the teacher is capable of promoting and encouraging whole-person learning. According to Rogers, this quality emphasizes a basic trust and belief that the student(s) are not only capable of learning but also capable of teaching.
- o **Empathetic understanding:** According to Rogers, this attribute refers to the teacher's ability to accurately decipher the student's **phenomenal field**. That is, the teacher understands the student's internal reactions and achieves a sensitive awareness of the mechanism of the process by which education and learning exert emotive impacts on the student

Carl Rogers opined that an Adult Learning Facilitator should perform the following tasks for ensuring the psychosocial well-being of the learners; -

- ✓ Setting a conducive climate for learning.
- ✓ Clarifying the purpose of learning to the learner(s),
- ✓ Leveraging and crafting instrumental learning resources and making them easily available to the learners
- ✓ Restoring and maintaining the intellectual and emotional components of learning,
- ✓ Exchanging feelings and thoughts with learners
- ✓ Abstain from the practice of dominating the learners

Carl Rogers affirmed that for ensuring effective facilitation of the comprehensive learning process

- o The students should participate completely in the learning process and should have control over its nature and direction,
- o Facilitation should be primarily based upon direct confrontation with practical, social, personal, or research problems
- o Self-evaluation should be the principal method of assessing progress or success.

The valued inputs of Carl Rogers are highly instrumental for Psychosocial Mentoring

Conclusion

Empowering the students through Mentoring is a gradual psychological process. Similarly developing a Higher Education Teacher into Mentor is also a gradual process. It has to be borne in mind that Mentor is not only a Subject Specialist . Rather , a Mentor should be an empathetic person with psychological and social sensitivity . A Mentor should empathize with the problems of the learners , be compassionate to them , and should have the resilience to select the appropriate strategic intervention that can enhance the psychological fortitude of the learners.

Our team is deeply engaged in the mission of developing Psycho-social Mentors . We are highly proactive to facilitate the transformation of Subject Matter Experts into Psycho-social Mentors .

We hope that this document will facilitate the Higher Education Teachers in achieving conceptual clarity regarding the Mentoring .

* * *

Prepared by

Dr. Srijani Ray

Assistant Professor in Philosophy

Dr.B.R.Ambedkar Satabarshiki Mahavidyalaya

CHAPTERS WITH RELEVANCE, RATIONALE AND SIGNIFICANCE

Mental Health and Wellbeing in Educational Settings

Keyword: **Introduction, What is mental health?,Mental health disorder,Connection between mental health and well-being,Relation between mental health and success in educational settings,Conclusion**

Introduction

This article wants to claim that a good mental health can achieve success in educational sector. To justify the claim at first one should know the definition of mental health, understand the connection between mental health and wellbeing and also the relation between mental health and success in educational settings. The World Health Organization (WHO) conceptualizes mental health as a "state of well-being in which the individual realizes his or her own abilities, can cope with the normal stresses of life, can work productively and fruitfully, and is able to make a contribution to his or her community". Mental health includes understanding and managing your emotions, thoughts, and overall mental state. It's the day-to-day experience of how you feel. According to the psychological perspective mental health is a state of mind characterized by emotional well-being, good behavioural adjustment, relative freedom from anxiety and disabling symptoms, and a capacity to establish constructive relationships and cope with the ordinary demands and stresses of life. The principle of mental health is ensuring all people have access to the same quality of care including early intervention care, that takes a holistic approach prevents an individual's condition from worsening is a crucial principle of mental health care. There are three types of factors which are affecting mental health. These are biological factor, psychological factor and social factor. Biological factors are physical health, genetics, diet, sleep, age etc. Psychological factors are beliefs, mental health diagnoses, perception, addictions etc. Social factors are relationships, family, culture, work, money, housing etc. Now the question is why is it called mental health? Mental wellness is viewed as a positive attribute; this definition of mental health highlights emotional well-being, the capacity to live a full and creative life, and the flexibility to deal with life's inevitable challenges.

What is mental health?

Now the question is why mental health is important in our day-to-day life? The World Health Organization (WHO) reports a sharp rise in the number of people experiencing mental illness in recent years, with the COVID-19 pandemic exacerbating mental health problems throughout the world. For students, it is more important than ever to address your mental health issues to stay mentally healthy and keep up with your educational and personal goals.

Even before the pandemic, mental health was a prominent concern for students. In 2019, the National College Health Assessment (NCHA) noted that many students reported feeling exhausted, lonely and overwhelmed, among other symptoms and difficulties. Of the surveyed students, 20.2% reported experiencing depression and 27.8% reported experiencing anxiety that affected their studies in the preceding year. Actually, while navigating educational and career goals and combatting personal challenges, your mental health hugely impacts the overall quality of your life. Therefore, mental health is important.

Mental health and psychosocial wellbeing are one of the most neglected areas in our country. The National Mental Health Survey (2016), reports almost one hundred fifty million citizens of our country needing care and support for their mental health wellbeing. Additionally, it was discovered that between seventy to ninety percent of these people failed to receive early, timely and quality intervention. According to World Health Organisation (WHO) the self-harm rates in the adolescent age group are found in the highest numbers at a global level. Emotional stress and other concerns are a major contributing factor for most of the physical illnesses. Mental healthcare providers like psychiatrists, clinical psychologists, counsellors and allied professionals agree that early intervention can prevent many future mental health conditions. Further research findings suggest that factors like physical illness, limited basic resources, inability to provide for self and family as well as unfulfilled desires in life are major factors that impact mental health and wellbeing.

Regarding this issue I want to quote the message of Mr. Dharmendra Pradhan, Minister of Education, Skill development and Entrepreneurship, Govt. of India. He said, "the importance of mental health and well-being, especially among school going students has been acknowledged by National Education Policy, 2020. He also said that as we are aware that the mental health is extremely important in schools as they have an essential role to play in supporting students to enable a state of well-being where students can meet their learning potential, cope with stress, and openly connect with their friends and community. It is in this context, 'Manodarpan' an initiative, was launched by the Ministry of Education under the AtmaNirbhar Bharat Abhiyan, to address mental health and well-being concerns of students. Along with various other activities, a mental health survey was conducted by the Manodarpan cell, NCERT on the students across the country. This is the first time that such a comprehensive survey on mental health of school-going children has been conducted. This survey will certainly be useful for teachers, educational administrators, policy makers and educationists while preparing and planning pragmatic policies and programmes focusing on enhancing the mental well-being of students which will foster their overall growth, well-being and happiness.

According to Anita Karwal, Secretary of the department of School Education & Literacy, Ministry of Education, Government of India, NEP 2020 emphasizes students' mental health and well-being in order to promote their holistic development. Mental well-being is interlinked with all aspects of health-physical, social and emotional.

The survey of Manodarpan was undertaken by the Ministry of education with the aim to gain an understanding of the perception of school students on different aspects of mental health and well-being. A total of 3,79,842 students participated in the survey between January to March,2022 from all states and union territories of the country. The survey throws light on the present-day reality of students in their personal, emotional, social life, challenges related to educational and career choices, dealing with the stress and anxiety related to competitions, academics, etc.

The significance of the survey is that it provides an understanding of factors affecting mental health more as contributing to well-being of students and, therefore, the findings have implications for efforts being made under the NEP,2020 to promote holistic development of the students.

Mental health issues among students have been a concern for policy makers. Therefore NEP. 2020 highlights the urgent need for ensuring not only cognitive development, but also building character and creating holistic and well-rounded individuals equipped with key 21st century skills. It is also vital that education nurtures the development of competencies such as communication,cooperation, team work and resilience among students.

To take forward the vision of NEP, Manodarpan, an initiative of the Ministry of Education as part of Atmanirbhar Bharat Abhiyan is aimed to provide psychological support to students, teachers and families for mental health and emotional well-being during the times of COVID-19 and beyond. The Manodarpan Cell, NCERT undertakes several activities which focus on extending support and addressing the mental health concerns like stress and anxiety of a target population.

Mental health disorder

Mental illness is a general term for a group of illnesses that may include symptoms that can affect a person's thinking, perceptions, mood or behaviour. Mental illness can make it difficult for someone to cope with work, relationships and other demands.

The relationship between stress and mental illness is complex, but it is known that stress can worsen an episode of mental illness. Most people can manage their mental illness with medication, counseling or both. This page lists some of the more common mental health issues and mental illnesses. Now I want to explain some mental health crisis.

Anxiety disorders

Anxiety disorders are a group of mental health problems. They include generalised anxiety disorders, social phobias, specific phobias (for example agoraphobia and claustrophobia), and panic disorders. Depression is often related to anxiety disorders.

Anxiety disorders are common mental health problems that affect many people. Approximately 25% of the population have an anxiety disorder that warrants treatment at some time in their life and up to another 25% have less severe anxieties such as fears of spider and snakes.

Behavioural and emotional disorders in children

All young children can be naughty, defiant and impulsive from time to time, which is perfectly normal. However, some children have extremely difficult and challenging behaviours that are outside the norm from their age. The most common disruptive behaviour disorders include oppositional defiant disorder (ODD), conduct disorder (CD) and attention deficit hyperactivity disorder (ADHD). These three behavioural disorders share some common symptoms, so diagnosis can be difficult and time consuming. A child or adolescent may have two disorders at the same time. Other exacerbating factors can include emotional problems, mood disorders, family difficulties and substance abuse.

Bipolar affective disorder

Bipolar affective disorder is a type of mood disorder, previously referred to as 'manic depression'. A person with bipolar disorder experiences episodes of mania (elation) and depression. The person may or may not experience psychotic symptoms. The exact cause is unknown, but a genetic predisposition has been clearly established. Environmental stressors can also trigger episodes of this mental illness.

Depression

Depression is a mood disorder characterised by lowering of mood, loss of interest and enjoyment, and reduced energy. It is not just feeling sad. There are different types and symptoms of depression. There are varying levels of severity and symptoms related to depression. Symptoms of depression can lead to increased risk of suicidal thoughts of behaviour.

Dissociation and dissociative disorders

Dissociation is a mental process where a person disconnects from their thoughts, feelings, memories or sense of identity. Dissociative disorders include dissociative amnesia, depersonalisation disorder and dissociative identity disorder.

Eating disorders

Eating disorders are serious mental illnesses. They can affect people of all age groups, genders, backgrounds, cultures, and in different body sizes. The number of people with eating disorders is increasing. Eating disorders are estimated to affect almost one million Australians. Some groups in the community are at greater risk, including females, children, and gender and sexually diverse people.

We understand more about eating disorders now than ever before. Yet, many people can live with an eating disorder for a long time without being diagnosed or accessing treatment. Seeking support from a professional as early as possible can help people to recover more quickly and reduce the impact of the eating disorder on the person's health and wellbeing.

Obsessive compulsive disorder

Obsessive compulsive disorder (OCD) is an anxiety disorder that affects two to three percent of the population (more than 500,000 Australians). It usually begins in late childhood or early adolescence. People with OCD experience recurrent and persistent thoughts, images or impulses that are intrusive and unwanted (obsessions). They also perform repetitive and ritualistic actions that are excessive, time-consuming and distressing (compulsions). People with OCD are usually aware of the irrational and excessive nature of their obsessions and compulsions. However, they feel unable to control their obsessions or resist their compulsions.

Paranoia

Paranoia is the irrational and persistent feeling that people are 'out to get you' or that you are the subject of persistent, intrusive attention by others.
This unfounded mistrust of others can make it difficult for a person with paranoia to function socially or have close relationships.

Paranoia may be a symptom of a number of conditions, including:
- paranoid personality disorder
- delusional (paranoid) disorder
- schizophrenia

Post-traumatic stress disorder

Post-traumatic stress disorder (PTSD) is a mental health condition that can develop as a response to people who have experienced any traumatic event. This can be a car or other serious accident, physical or sexual assault, war-related events or torture, or natural disasters such as bushfires or floods.

Psychosis

People affected by psychosis can experience delusions, hallucinations and confused thinking. Psychosis can occur in a number of mental illnesses, including drug-induced psychosis, schizophrenia and mood disorders. Medication and psychological support can relieve, or even eliminate, psychotic symptoms.

Schizophrenia

Schizophrenia is a complex brain disorder, which affects about one in a 100 or between 150,000 and 200,000 Australians. The illness is characterised by disruptions to thinking and emotions, and a distorted perception of reality. It usually begins in late adolescence or early adulthood and does not spare any race, culture, class or sex. About 20 to 30 per cent of people with schizophrenia experience only a few brief episodes. For others, it is a chronic condition. Ten per cent of people with schizophrenia commit suicide.

Connection between mental health and well-being

After the discussion of mental health disorder, I want to relate mental health with the well-being in educational settings.

Schools and family are important social units which anchor the health and well-being of all individuals. Schools have the prime responsibility to promote and optimize the physical, social and also the mental health of students. The emerging challenges have necessitated that the schools also shift the focus to the psychosocial needs of students and take care of the overall wellbeing. Identification and Prevention can essentially create safe ecosystems. Perhaps this article will focus to align the role and importance of, parents, schools, teachers, counsellors, special educators as immediate care givers at different developmental phases of students.

Further research findings suggest that factors like physical illness, limited basic resources, inability to provide for self and family as well as unfulfilled desires in life are major factors that impact mental health and wellbeing.

A holistically healthy individual engages in productive activities, has fulfilling relationships with others, and displays the capacity to adapt to change and cope with adversity.

Relation between mental health and success in educational settings

To ensure physical and psychological safety of our children, easy access to mental health service and support in schools is the first step. The ambit of mental health must encompass the emotional, behavioural, and social wellbeing of a child. The most important feature of mental health is 'adaptability', the ability to cope with daily life challenges effectively. Giving a secure environment to children in schools is important for this reason. Easy access, wellbeing and adaptability must be aligned together to create a comprehensive system in a school.

1. Positive Mental Health= Success in Life

   Children's success in school and life is directly linked to their mental health. Some research findings indicate that children who receive mental health support do better in academics, are flexible and adaptive to change. The overall mental health determines learning. Problem in activities and behaviour can be addressed by providing mental health support.

2. Reason for Growing Need

   Research suggests that almost one-fifth of the children and adolescents experience a mental health concern like stress, anxiety, bullying, learning disability, and/or alcohol and substance abuse. A large number of students do not receive the attention and care they need because of the prevalent stigma associated with mental illnesses. Therefore, it is important to have widespread awareness to address the mental health challenges faced by school students.

3. Need for Trained Professionals

School counselors are specifically trained to handle behavioural and emotional challenges faced by children and adolescents. They are attuned to understand the struggles of students. Teachers also receive practical training in child development.

Access to mental health services in schools is vital in improving the physical and psychological safety of students and schools. It is important to create a school culture that enables the student to report safety concerns. School mental health professionals provide support, identify and work with students over more intense or ongoing needs.

One of the most important challenges is accepting and adapting to change and a child is expected to adapt to various challenges s/he experiences while growing up. We are raised to believe that change is the only constant in life. Transitions are an essential part of our life and they come in various life situations, starting from our childhood. Hence, transition from child's perspective can be very challenging. For example, some children at pre-primary grade level at times feel insecure when they are expected to adapt to another setting and routine in primary school. Most of the time we do not look at it as an issue and assume that the child will adjust to these changes. In most cases, this transition from home to school can be smooth for the child, but in some cases, it might be disturbing if not handled with care. During the early developmental years, the child shows changes in the physical, motor, social, emotional, language, and cognitive skills. The role of families and parents is to ensure school readiness. Teachers with the support of families ensure within school transitions.

Family is the first socialization framework the child is exposed to. It is an important cornerstone for a child because attachment, emotions, personality traits, behaviours emanate from the family. Right from food preference to interest and social interaction all depend on this one unit. The next framework of socialization is school. This provides plethora of opportunities and psychological space for holistic development. Community, from a developmental perspective has a broader meaning. It may include the teachers connected over a period of an academic year. It may imply the families and neighbourhood for the psychosocial support. In short, it includes various places where children feel affiliated to and have a feeling of belongingness. Children's relationship with environment starts from the family and gradually encompasses people outside. Teachers are a significant part of this relationship. Conclusively, family, schools and communities together work hand in hand in fostering the mental health and wellbeing of the child. They are equal stakeholders in the upbringing of the child.

Almost all children attend school and spend 6-7 hours of their time every day in that learning environment. Incorporating mental health into the school curriculum can have substantial influence on well-being of the students. A school that makes conscious effort to constantly promote mental health and wellbeing of its children strengthens its capacity as a healthy setting for living and learning. The increase in the reports of bullying and school violence emphasizes the importance of early recognition and response to the situations. In the last decade, school mental health has expanded to address school violence, bullying, substance abuse, discrimination and maintaining healthy discipline. The priority in schools should mainly be about early identification at the individual and systemic level. There are two main goals here- bringing positive change to a children's behaviour and optimizing their potential academically. It also focusses on preventing future negative outcomes for children. Hence, the school counselling program and policy are collaborative efforts having benefits for students and their multiple stake holders in a school setup i.e. parents, teachers, administration and management. This is the responsibility of schools.

Family is the most valuable source of support for children. It includes parents, siblings, grandparents, close relatives, especially when we are looking at the collectivistic culture quintessential to our country. In all the stages of life, the family support shows dynamic changes. For e.g., in healthy and functional families, during childhood, the children are completely dependent on all their needs on the family. As the child grows up, this dependence tends to modify. There is a growing consensus about the positive influence of grandparents on their grandchildren's development and, consequently, on their mental health. The scenario of multigenerational families is a crucial part of the societal fabric of India. Growing-up years are often associated to 'nani ki kahaani' and 'dadi ke nuskhe'. Grandparents offer love, guidance and wisdom. Research indicates, "with changing family patterns, increased life expectancy, growing numbers of dual-worker households and higher rates of family breakdown, grandparents are now playing an increasing role in their grandchildren's lives". Hence, the concept of multigenerational families entails unconditional love, shared responsibilities, safety and security. Parent-child relationships can be complex. If the child is experiencing emotional and behavioural difficulties, managing for parents may be difficult at times. A parent must take care and be patient, regularly spend quality time with the child and consult counselors and other mental health professionals about possible interventions. This is the responsibility of family.

As the term 'community' is vast in its scope, some examples were mentioned before. Keeping the essence of the term intact, community is anything that the child feels belonged to and derives a sense safety and support. The feeling of support and safety gives them the confidence to play, explore and learn. Hence, connection to the community creates a responsive, safe, and stable education and caring environment. Communities foster positive interactions and relationships between children, peers, and adults and strengthen outcomes.

Schools provide a comprehensive framework that includes learning opportunities for students and the promotion of growth on all fronts- physical, emotional, psychological, and social. Teachers are one of the most crucial linkages to the positive mental health of students. They play a significant role in a student's life. They are embodiments of knowledge, moral support, encouragement and love. Teachers have a crucial role in shaping a student's future; they make students independent. Essentially, a teacher offers learning support, innovates around the teaching aids and facilitates all possible guidance. At the classroom level, teachers can aid guidance and support by showing empathy for the students' personal, emotional or family related problems. One can try to understand the reasons which form the base for some students' emotional disorders and their deviant behaviours. Having non-judgemental and unmasked communication with students may also help them tremendously. In many situations, a healthy and communicative relationship between the teacher and a student helps identify behavioural deviations and emotional conflicts, hence preventing a significant number of concerns. After understanding a problem faced by a student, the role of a teacher is to help students to enable them and facilitate them to solve the problem independently. Such facilitation works on the principle that every individual, if guided properly, can develop better-coping skills. Empathy is considered as one of the most important skills for a teacher. Teacher addresses problems related to the school and beyond school. A teacher may not replace or substitute the expertise of a counselor, but in the absence of a trained counsellor, can don the role of a substitute help. A teacher would be the first to be able to raise the alarm and reach out to the counsellor or any mental health professional associated with the school if s/ he or she notices any unhealthy emotions or behavioural manifestations. The teacher-counsellor team would then be able to collaborate and work closely to help the child in situations as soon as the teacher notices.

There is a growing importance of School Counselors as an important part of the educational leadership team as they provide valuable assistance to students. The complexities that exist in a school set up because a child is spending his maximum waking hours in school makes it important to have trained and dedicated counselors working towards students' mental health. Counseling helps students in the following ways

- Change maladaptive and unhealthy behavioural manifestations to adaptive and healthy ones.
- Build time management and organizational skills
- Establishing clear academic goals
- Resolving interpersonal problems and fostering positive group behaviour
- Conflict resolution
- Enhancing self-esteem
- Working through personal problems which cause emotional distress

Every Secondary and Senior Secondary School should appoint a person on full time basis for performing the duties of Special Educator. The appointment and qualifications of Special Educator shall be in accordance with guidelines laid down by the Board and the minimum requirement laid down by Rehabilitation Council of India in this regard. Special Educators are essentially case managers/ experts and are responsible for the development, implementation, and evaluation of students' Individualized Educational Programs. Such Individualized Educational Program are specific and unique curriculum objectives which are made keeping in mind the individual student's needs. Special Educators mainly provide the necessary information about special students, their needs, disability, medical concerns, equipment operation to the classroom teacher in advance. They essentially collaborate with teachers in adapting the curriculum, providing appropriate modifications, ensuring the implementation, and assessing overall progress of special students.

Conclusion

The mind is a vital organ that influences the entire body's functioning. When mental health is compromised, it can impact overall bodily functions. Achieving success in all areas of life requires both physical and emotional fitness. Students' mental health and well-being is very much supported by schools. Schools try to promote mental health awareness and resources. Schools can help these students with interventions, support groups, and therapies. These resources can help reduce the negative impact on mental health. Students who prioritise their mental health are better able to manage stress, anxiety, and depression, which can lead to better academic performance. Better relationships: Good mental health can lead to improved social connections and better relationships with peers, family, and friends. Education offers opportunities to learn more about health and health risks, both in the form of health education in the school curriculum and by giving individuals the health literacy to draw on, later in life, and absorb messages about important lifestyle choices to prevent or manage diseases. Because of misconceptions and stigma surrounding mental health issues, people often suffer in silence and don't seek treatment for their conditions. Mental health awareness is an important initiative to improve understanding of mental health conditions and increase access to healthcare for those who need it. Education can also lead to more accurate health beliefs and knowledge, and thus to better lifestyle choices, but also to better skills and greater self-advocacy. Education improves skills such as literacy, develops effective habits, and may improve cognitive ability.

REFERENCES:

1. "Exploring Happiness: From Aristotle to Brain Science" by S. Bok (2010),Yale University Press.

2. "An Agenda for India's Growth: Essays in Honour of P Chidambaram" edited by Sameer Kochhar

3. "The Gifts of Perfection" (K. Neff, 2011) HarperCollins.

4. "Play Therapy" by J. Lamotte and K. Smith in "Assessing and Treating Youth Exposed to Traumatic Stress" edited by V. Carrion would be cited as: Lamotte, J., & Smith, K. (2019). Play therapy. In V. Carrion (Ed.), Assessing and treating youth exposed to traumatic stress (pp. 129-140). American Psychiatric Association

5. "Mental Health and High School Curriculum Guide" (Kutcher, Wei, & Morgan, 2015)

6. "Teaching Students with Anxiety" (Moreillon, 2020)

7. "The Social Skills Guidebook" (Bishop, 2018)

8. "The Whole-Brain Child" (Siegel & Bryson, 2011)

9. "Teaching Students with Anxiety" (Moreillon, 2020)

Inclusive Education and Diversity

Shri. Suvankar Biswas

SACT-I, Dept. of Education,
Dr. B. R. Ambedkar Satabarshiki Mahavidyalaya,
Helencha, Bagdah, N 24 Pgs, West Bengal.

Abstract: Inclusive education and diversity are interconnected concepts central to building equitable and just societies. Together, they emphasize the importance of embracing differences, fostering an environment and providing equal opportunities where all individuals feel valued and respected. In India, there are many diverse communities, customs, cultures, and languages, which makes promoting inclusive education and diversity in the educational institutions a critical task. Inclusive Education includes teaching strategies, curriculum and classroom environment to meet the diverse needs of students. This may include the use of Assistive Technology, individualized education plans (IEPs), and Differentiated Instruction. Collaborative efforts between teachers, parents and experts are integral to its success. However, this will require clear laws, plans, government-private-social and personal support and responsibilities. This paper or article introduces important insights from educational psychology on how to use diversity to help students feel at home in their learning environment, encourage students to challenge assumptions, enhance critical thinking, and design education to suit different student needs.

Keywords: Inclusion, inclusive education, diversity.

Introduction:

Inclusive education and diversity are essential components of an effective and successful education system in the country. In country of India, there are many diverse communities, customs, cultures, and languages, which makes promoting inclusive education and diversity in the educational institutions a critical task. India is the most diverse country in the world. And unity in diversity is the main feature of the country. It has been flowing since ancient times. This mantra continues to resonate in the sky and air of the country. For this diversity, Historian **Vincent Smith** has described Indian civilization as **"Unity in the midst of diversity"**.

In India this diversity is spread over a vast land from Kashmir to Kanyakumari, with extraordinary geographical diversity in terms of temperature, climate, biological and plant diversity, human diversity, linguistic diversity, religious diversity, etc., as well as this diversity exists in education or students. If all the people of the country do not respect this diversity, if everyone does not have pride in this diversity, then the ability to unite in diversity will not be as effective in advancing universal education in the country. And to expand this education everywhere, the expansion of inclusive education is urgently needed. The education system of the country is mainly designed keeping the average child in mind. Such a system cannot meet the special needs of a child born with a disability or with greater abilities than normal children of the same age, or who is brought up in a different culture or environment. Inclusion plans have tried to assimilate all these needs into the average needs.

The range of diversity is widened when social groups are identified as marginal. To solve these problems it is important to use different techniques recognized and accepted by the society. Diversity is not just a descriptive term; it refers to an ideological stance that values and respects cultural pluralism and advocates its preservation within society. The concept of diversity includes acceptance and respect for members of a group. It is loaded with a political perspective positively inclined towards justice and equity in society.

Meaning of Inclusion:

Inclusion refers to a particular philosophy that believes that all people are equal, respected and valuable. It extends beyond the school classroom to the larger society and life, where every human being is an equal participant. It is an ongoing and never-ending process, where any individual, child or adult, can participate equally in all activities of society. Therefore, in schools, children, regardless of their race, religion, culture, gender or disability can study together and can receive special equipment, special instruction or specially trained teachers as needed. Inclusion refers to the provision of all children in school to their fullest potential. It refers to the acceptance of children by all and their equality with each other.

Inclusion is an educational practice in which students with special needs are fully integrated into the general education classroom of a school. The philosophy of inclusion is based on the idea that every individual, regardless of their disability, has the right to be fully included in the fabric of society. Research conducted on inclusive classrooms shows benefits for both traditional and special needs students. Some of the definitions are-

Booth (1996): "Inclusion is a process that increases participation in education and reduces exclusion from educational opportunities".

Anita et.al (2002): "Inclusion is when a student with a disability is unconditionally given the opportunity to participate in the classroom and group of a traditional school".

Meaning of Inclusive Education:

The concept of inclusive education is rooted in the principles of equity, equality and social justice. It seeks to remove barriers that prevent students from learning and progressing within mainstream educational settings. This includes addressing differences in physical, cognitive, emotional, social, or linguistic abilities as well as cultural and socioeconomic inequalities.

Inclusive education is an approach to teaching and learning that embraces diversity by ensuring that all students, regardless of their abilities, disabilities or backgrounds, have equitable access to quality education. It emphasizes creating a supportive learning environment where each student feels valued, respected and empowered to participate fully in the educational process.

Inclusive Education is a step towards building an inclusive and equitable society, guided by international frameworks such as the United Nations Sustainable Development Goals (SDG-4) and National Policies. It reinforces the belief that every child, regardless of their situation, has the right to learn and achieve their full potential.

In practice, Inclusive Education includes teaching strategies, curriculum and classroom environment to meet the diverse needs of students. This may include the use of Assistive Technology, individualized education plans (IEPs), and Differentiated Instruction. Collaborative efforts between teachers, parents and experts are integral to its success.

Definitions of Inclusive Education:

Inclusive education does not only benefit students with special needs but also fosters empathy, cooperation and mutual respect among all students. It prepares individuals to live and work in different communities, promotes a culture of acceptance and reduces social inequality. Regarding the definitions of Inclusive Education,

Advani and Chadha (2003) said, "Inclusive education aims to provide a favorable setting for achieving equal opportunity and full participation for all thus bringing children with special needs well within the preview of mainstreaming education. It recognizes …….. without disabilities learn together".

According to **M Manivanan (2001),** "Inclusive education is the implementation of the policy and process that allows all children to participate in all programmes…..".

According to **Norwich (1999),** "All children who are in any way Inclusive education is about giving them social recognition and opportunities to learn according to their individual needs, even though they have some disabilities, in other respects they are just like any other normal student".

Professor Michael F Giangreco (1997) said, "Inclusive education is a set of values' principles and practice that seeks more effective and meaningful education for all students, regardless of whether they have exceptionality labels or not".

Objectives of Inclusive Education:

Inclusion of children with disabilities is of great importance in the field of education. Some of the special needs of children with disabilities are met through Inclusive Education. Therefore, inclusion in the field of education definitely has some objectives. These objectives are-

1. To give importance to meeting the specific educational needs of the child rather than the class standard.
2. To provide more careful education to children with mild disabilities in a minimally controlled environment.

3. To determine ways to improve the mentality of normal students in general classes towards their fellow disabled children and to form a cooperative attitude.
4. To gradually reduce social distance through equal distribution of various facilities and on the basis of mutual understanding.
5. To develop various social qualities in these children.
6. To engage various educationists and experts to improve the teaching methods, learning process, etc.
7. To remove the frustration and inferiority complex of disabled students.

Meaning and Concept of Diversity:

Diversity refers to the presence and recognition of differences between individuals or groups in characteristics such as race, gender, age, socioeconomic status, religion, ability, sexual orientation, education, and cultural background. It incorporates the unique perspectives, experiences and identities that people bring to a community or organization, creating a rich tapestry of human diversity.

The idea of diversity goes beyond mere presentation; it emphasizes inclusion, respect, and equal opportunity for all. It recognizes that every person has inherent worth and that embracing difference can lead to a more harmonious and productive society. Diversity enhances innovation, creativity, and adaptability by allowing individuals to learn from each other's experiences and perspectives.

In education, the workplace, and social contexts, diversity creates environments where all individuals feel valued and respected, free from discrimination or prejudice. It also includes identifying and addressing systemic barriers that may prevent certain groups from fully participating in social structures.

Diversity plays a key role in promoting social cohesion and reducing prejudice. By encouraging open-mindedness and understanding, it helps to bridge cultural and ideological gaps by encouraging peaceful coexistence.

Diversity means more than recognizing or tolerating difference or both ideas. Diversity is a set of conscious practices that involve-

1. Understanding and appreciating the interdependence between humanity, culture, and the natural environment.
2. Practicing mutual respect for the qualities and experiences that are different from our own.
3. Understanding that diversity includes not only ways of being but also ways of knowing.
4. Recognizing the personal, cultural, and institutional recognition that creates and maintains inequality and privileges for others creates and maintains inequality for others.
5. Building alliances across differences so that it can work together to eliminate all forms of inequality.

In a globalized world, diversity is being viewed as strength rather than a challenge. It prepares individuals to navigate a complex, interconnected society and underscores the importance of empathy, cooperation, and mutual respect. Ultimately, embracing diversity means celebrating the richness of human experience and ensuring equal status for all.

Definition of Diversity:

According to **UNESCO**, "Diversity is the multiplicity of identities, cultures, and perspectives present in a community or organization, which contributes to the richness and dynamism of society".

According to **Williams, D. A. (2013)**, "Diversity is each of us and all of us, individually and collectively. Diversity is all that makes each of us different and those things that all resemble us".

According to **Cambridge Dictionary**, "Diversity is defined as "the fact of many different types of things or people being included in something; a range of different things or people".

According to **Educational Context**, "Diversity in education involves the presence of students from different ethnic, cultural, socio-economic and linguistic backgrounds, promoting inclusive learning environments that respect and integrate these differences".

According to **Social Perspective**, "Diversity is the acceptance and inclusion of people who differ in their identities, experiences or beliefs, ensuring equal opportunity and reducing discrimination or prejudice".

These definitions highlight diversity as a concept rooted in the recognition and celebration of difference while encouraging inclusion and equality.

Inclusive Education and Diversity:

Inclusive education and diversity are interconnected concepts central to building equitable and just societies. Together, they emphasize the importance of embracing differences, fostering an environment and providing equal opportunities where all individuals feel valued and respected.

Inclusive education is a teaching approach that ensures that all students, regardless of their abilities, disabilities, backgrounds, or learning needs, have access to quality education within the mainstream classroom. In the context of Diversity includes the range of differences that exist between groups and individual, including gender, race, age, ability, ethnicity, religion, linguistic, socio-economic status, and cultural.

The classroom is a representative sample of society that reflects the diversity of people in the community. The growing number of students from diverse backgrounds enrolling in primary grades has reinforced the importance of making schools more inclusive. With relatively greater diversity in student talent and social, cultural, economic, and political backgrounds, a teacher is expected to transfer understandings and positions on diversity to classroom processes, identifying and recognizing threads of diversity among students to address related issues. Challenges related to curriculum design, teaching-learning practices and processes and learning materials, in order to subsequently meet the diverse learning needs of children. In particular, the primary class in India faces the enormous challenge of constructively weaving diversity into class processes in order to democratize these processes and practices, all geared toward the larger goal of social justice.

The importance of the **"Inclusive Education"** agenda has been further reinforced by the enactment of the **Right of Children to Free and Compulsory Education (RTE) Act, 2009** and the **Rights of Persons with Disabilities Act, 2016.**

Need of Inclusive Education:

In almost all the countries of the world, inclusive education has gained special importance. Education has changed from exclusionary to inclusive education. Therefore, inclusive education has a special need in the modern education and social system. For example-

1. Education is the fundamental right of every child. Every child has the right to quality education and learning. Therefore, inclusive education is necessary to provide every child with the opportunity to achieve and maintain an acceptable level of education.
2. This education is necessary for learning according to the unique characteristics, interests and abilities of each child.
3. This education is necessary to take into account the different characteristics and needs of children.
4. This education is necessary for those with special educational needs to achieve the goal of going to school every day.
5. This education is necessary to develop personality traits in children.
6. This education is necessary to instill moral values in children and educate them for life preparation.
7. This education is necessary for the effective and efficient use of human resources and educational resources.

CONCLUSION:

The Inclusive Education is to create a general education system where all types of children with special needs (blind, deaf, speech-impaired, intellectually disabled, muscular and neurologically disabled, brain-related disabilities, self-absorbed children, socio-economically, culturally backward children, children from marginalized groups, neglected children on streets and sidewalks, children born and brought up in brothels) included in the general education system and their families receive the same quality of education as their peers in nearby schools. For this, possible desirable changes should be made in the school infrastructure, administrative system, teacher training, teacher selection, evaluation and curriculum design and teachers should develop all kinds of teaching skills in such a way that they are able to teach all kinds of special needs children in regular school classrooms with everyone and promote the same quality. They may sometimes need a little help from special teachers or they can succeed in this task without the help of special teachers. For this, all teacher training courses should provide a detailed and clear understanding of the education of children with special needs.

Such an inclusive school concept will take effect only when all regular school teachers are able to understand and meet the educational needs of all children with special needs. However, this will require clear laws, plans, government-private-social and personal support and responsibilities.

REFERENCES:

From Books:

1. Ainscow, M. (1999). *Understanding the Development of Inclusive Schools.* Falmer Press, London.
2. Booth, T. and Ainscow, M. (2011). *Index for inclusion: Developing learning and participation in schools.* CSIE, Bristol.
3. Chatterjee, M., Pal, A.K. and Pandey, P. (2019-20). *Educational Sociology.* Rita Publication, Kolkata.
4. Debnath, D. and Pal, A.K. (2021-22). *Special Education.* Rita Publication, Kolkata.
5. Jhingran, D. (2009). *Hundreds of home languages in the country and many in most classrooms: Coping with diversity in primary education in India, Social justice through multilingual education,* (pp. 263-282).
6. Mangal, S. K. (2012). *Educating exceptional children: An Introduction to special education.* PHI Learning, Delhi.
7. Oliver M. The social model in action: If I had a hammer, Barnes C, Mercer G. (Eds.). Implementing the social model of disability: Theory and research, Leeds 2004, (pp. 18-31).
8. Oliver M. (1990). *The politics of disablement.* Basingstoke Macmillan.
9. Roy, P. and Roy, A. (2017). *Creating an Inclusive Education.* Rita Book Agency, Kolkata.
10. Shakespeare T, Erickson, M. (2000). *Social Work: Introducing Professional Practice, Higham.* Sage. London (pp. 169).

From Websites:

1. Albert, B. The social model of disability, human rights and development 2004. Retrieved from
http://www.enil.eu/wp-content/uploads/2012/ 07/Thesocial-model-of-disability-human-rights-development-2004.pdf

2. Barnes, C. Re-thinking disability, work and welfare. Sociology Compass 2012; 6(6):472-484. Retrieved from
http://pf7d7vi404s1dxh27mla5569.wpengine.netdnacdn.com/files/library/DisabilityWork-and-Welfare.pdf

3. Barton, Len. Inclusive education and teacher education 2003. Retrieved from
http://disabilitystudies.leeds.ac.uk/files/library/Bartoninclusiveeducation.pdf

4. Disability – Human Rights based model versus the Social, Medical and Charity models. Retrieved from
http://www.cutsinternational.org/cart/pdf/disability_junction_03-2011.pdf)://www.cutsinternational.org/cart/pdf/disability_junction_03-2011.pdf

5. Concept of Inclusive Education Retrieved from
https://www.unicef.org/education/inclusive-education

6. Concept of Inclusive Education Retrieved from
https://www.entab.in/How-to-Promote-Inclusive-Education.html

Experiential Learning Author

Dr. Keya Chakraborty,
SACT-1, Bengali Department ,
Dr. B.R Ambedkar Satabarshiki Mahavidyalaya

Experiential learning is a learning paradigm that provides an alternative to more traditional learning models.

Experiential learning is the idea that experiences are generated through our ongoing interactions and engagement with the world around us, and learning is an inevitable product of experience.

David Kolb's Experiential Learning Theory (ELT)

David Kolb's Experiential Learning Theory (ELT) is a foundational model in the field of education, psychology, and organizational development, emphasizing that learning is a process where knowledge is created through the transformation of experience.

Key Components of Kolb's Experiential Learning Theory

The Learning Cycle: Kolb proposed that Experiential Learning is a cyclic process involving four stages.

Stages of the Learning Cycle	Description	Example
Concrete Experience (CE):	✓ The cycle begins with the learners having a concrete experience – this implies incurring some tangible experience from any new activity, with which they were not acquainted earlier.	✓ A learner is exposed to a Game on Strategic Management. ✓ After the completion of the game, the learner incurs concrete experiences in Managerial Strategies.
Reflective Observation (RO):	✓ After the experience, the learner reflects on what happened. ✓ This stage involves cogitative reflection on the activities that triggered the experiences and analyzing the experiences.	✓ The learner reflects on the Management Game as well as on the experiences that he has incurred while playing the Game. ✓ He initiated the process of analyzing the experience incurred by him.

Abstract Conceptualization (AC):	✓ In this phase, the learners develop concepts based on the reflection. ✓ To be precise, they integrate the cognitive outcome of their reflections on experience with their existing knowledge and form new concepts.	✓ The learner integrated the cognitive outcome of his deep reflections, with his existing knowledge of Strategies. ✓ Eventually, the concept of a new strategy gets crystallized in his cognition.
Active Experimentation (AE):	✓ In this phase, the learners implement their abstract concepts in practical situations and appraise the outcome of the implementation. ✓ As a result, they incur concrete experiences. ✓ Thus, a new Experiential Learning Cycle starts.	✓ The learner administered his concept on the new strategy for solving a problem of absenteeism, dissatisfaction, non-engagement, and low morale of some employees, in a specific organizational matrix. ✓ While implementing the newly conceptualized strategy for alleviating the aforementioned problems, the learners incur new concrete experiences. ✓ Eventually, the learner enters into a new Experiential Learning Cycle.

Four Experiential Learning Styles Opined by David Kolb:

Kolb identified that individuals emanate preferences towards different ways of learning, which aligns with the combinations of the four stages of the learning cycle. He enumerated four primary learning styles based on the combination of the two dimensions:

- Diverging: (Concrete Experience + Reflective Observation)
  - Learners who prefer to view and analyze situations from multiple perspectives. They are reflective and creative. They are capable of multifarious creative ideas through profound cogitation.
- Assimilating: (Abstract Conceptualization + Reflective Observation)
  - Learners who emanate proclivity towards a logical approach. They are capable of integrating the cognitive outcome of deep reflection and their existing knowledge. Based on this cognitive integration, they develop conceptual models. They are proficient in integrating information with their existing knowledge for developing theoretical models.
- Converging: (Abstract Conceptualization + Active Experimentation)
  - Learners who emanate preference towards judicious application of ideas in the practical field, with an experimental approach. They translate abstract ideas into practice for the execution of critical tasks and the mitigation of practical problems. They are marked by their pragmatic mindset of verifying the efficacy of ideas in the matrix of practical reality.
- Accommodating: (Concrete Experience + Active Experimentation)
  - These are the Learners who prefer hands-on activities and tend to learn from the Concrete experiences incurred while executing the hands-on activities. They rely on the linear chain of; -

    "Activity-Consequence-Experience-Learning"

Steps of "Experiential Learning Process" aligning with Cognitive and Metacognitive Perspective

Recall	✓ The learners recall the Experiences incurred by them
Comprehension	✓ Through deep reflection, the learners comprehend the subtleties and intricacies of the experiences incurred by them.
Application through Documentation	✓ The comprehended elements of the experience are meticulously documented by the learners.
Analysis	✓ The learners critically analyze the documented experiences.
Evaluation	✓ The learner evaluates each of the components of Experience and gradually infers which components of the overall experience are more instrumental to their learning and development.
Creation of new concepts	✓ The learners integrate the selected experiences with their existing knowledge and develop new Concepts.
Active Experimentation	✓ The learners apply the new concepts (acquired through the integration of new experiences and existing knowledge) in practical situations to achieve pre-determined outcomes. ✓ The application of new concepts is made on an Experimental Basis.
Concrete Experience	✓ If some of the learners achieve the desired outcome, then they incur the concrete experience of success. ✓ If some of the learners fail to achieve the desired outcome, then they incur the concrete experience of failure. ✓ Eventually, the concrete experience of success initiates a new Experiential Learning Cycle. ✓ On the contrary, the concrete experience of failure initiates a different type of Experiential Learning Cycle.

Relationship between Inductive Pedagogy and Experiential Learning Model

Michael Prince and Richard Felder have established a relationship between the Inductive Learning Cycle and the Experiential Learning Model of David Kolb.

The following points establish the linkage between the Inductive approach and the Experiential Learning Model of David Kolb.

1	Introducing a problem and providing motivation for solving it by relating it to students' interests and experiences. Here the focal theme revolves around the "Why" Factor.
2	Presenting pertinent facts, experimental observations, principles and theories, problem-solving methods, etc., and opportunities for the students to reflect on them Here the focal theme revolves around the "What" Factor.
3	Providing guided hands-on practice in the methods and types of thinking the lessons are intended to teach Here the focal theme revolves around the "How" Factor.
4	Allowing and encouraging exploration of consequences and applications of the newly learned material Here the focal theme revolves around the "What if" Factor.

CONCLUSION:

Cause-Effect Relationship Dynamics between Inductive Pedagogy and Experiential Learning

Inductive pedagogy fosters experiential learning by putting students in practical situations where they get engaged directly with critical problems and challenging tasks, analyze them, create need-based strategies, formulate strategic action plans, execute strategic tasks, evaluate their pattern of execution, identify process gaps, and builds stratagems for replenishing the gaps.

While executing the aforementioned activities the learners incur diversified experiences. They reflect and analyze their experiences and draw new cognitive outputs/deductions from their reflections.

Subsequently, they integrate the new cognitive deductions with their existing knowledge and develop a new concept.

Thus, it is distinctly evident that Inductive Pedagogy fosters Experiential Learning.

ACKNOWLEDGEMENT

"Instructional Design & Learner Experience design"

Written by

Mr. Purandar Sengupta,

Dr. Venkateswara Rao Mannem,

DFr. Papiya upadhyay and

Dr. Rajdeep Deb